Selected Acathistos Hymns in Honour of the Theotokos

Gozalov Books
The Hague

This book has the blessing of
His Eminence Simon, Archbishop of Brussels and Belgium

ISBN: 978-90-79889-80-8; 9789079889808

Editor: Hegumena Lydia, Mother Superior of the Convent of the Mother of God Portaïtissa, Trazegnies, Belgium
Translators: Guram Kochi and Marijcke Tooneman, The Hague, Holland
Design: Guram Kochi and Marijcke Tooneman

© Gozalov Books, The Hague, 2024
Tel.: +31 70 352 15 65
E-mail: gozalovbooks@planet.nl
Website: www.hetsmallepad.nl

All rights reserved. No part of this publication may be reproduced or transmitted in any form or by any means, electronic or mechanical, including photocopy and recording, or stored in a retrieval system, without the written permission of the publisher.

Table of Contents

Foreword 5

Akathistos hymn in Honour of the Icon of the
Theotokos 'She Who mollifies the wicked Hearts' 9

Akathistos hymn in Honour of the Icon of the
Theotokos 'The Increase of Intelligence' 23

Akathistos hymn in Honour of the icon
of the Theotokos 'The protective Veil' 42

Akathistos hymn in Honour of the Icon of the
Theotokos 'Smolenskaya' or 'Hodigitria'
(She who shows the way) 58

Akathistos hymn in Honour of the icon of the
Theotokos 'Unfading Blossom' 76

Akathistos Hymn in Honour of the icon of the
Theotokos 'The Unconsumed burning Bush' 93

Akathistos hymn in Honour of the icon of the
Theotokos 'The Joy of All Who sorrow' 112

The History of the Icons 128

Foreword

Praying Acathistos hymns is a widely spread and cherished custom of Orthodox Christians. Many of them add an Acathistos either of their own choice, or according to their specific needs or upon the advice of their spiritual father, to their morning or evening prayers. However, it's rather difficult for those who do not master Church-Slavonic or Byzantine Greek to understand what exactly is said or meant in the Acathistos. Therefore this book is a big enrichment, allowing them as well as those who want to become acquainted with this exceptional form of Orthodox devotion to read and to pray several of the best known and most often used Acathistos-hymns in a modern language. Upon the request of His Eminence Simon, Archbishop of Brussels and Belgium and of The Hague and the Netherlands, only hymns originating from before the October revolution and which therefore are better known and enjoy greater venerability have been selected for this book.

Some of these hymns have a strong poetical expression, and most of all, a deep theological insight. Other hymns are the joyful cries of exultation of a believing soul singing her gratefulness to the Mother of God for the received blessings.

Every Orthodox soul wishes to praise the Most Holy Mother of God as much as is it is in her power, because she is the Protector of the Christians, always ready to help those who call upon her; a bulwark and guard for those who are in need and in sorrow; a fortress against the attacks of the passions and a shield in the battle against the demons.

Hence the Orthodox Church sings the praises of the Queen of Heaven and earth in so many hymns, songs and poems.

By praying the Acathistos hymns a Christian learns not only to resort to her, but also to trust in her Divine help. He doesn't go round in circles moaning about his problems, but instead elevates his soul in a song of joy for Christ's great work of Salvation, when He was incarnated in the virginal womb of Mary. Thus the soul gives "true honour" to God by extolling the Mother of the Son. And he, who has once tasted the joy of praising her, will discover her strength and power in a direct and miraculous way.

That's why many spiritual Fathers prompt their spiritual sons and daughters to pray these Acathistos hymns to the Mother of God, because in this way Christians experience the Divine might and Mary's protection against both demonic temptations and the wild passions which can try to seize man. Those for whom praying an Acathistos seems too long, may split it in two, so that they will sing praises in the morning as well as in the afternoon.

Seven hymns have been translated and offered to the praying believer:

1. Acathistos hymn in honour of the icon of the Mother of God "She who mollifies the wicked hearts". The author is unknown. Composed probably at the end of the 19th century.
2. Acathistos hymn in honour of the icon of the Mother of God "The Increase of Intelligence". The author is unknown. Composed probably at the end of the 19th century.
3. Acathistos hymn in honour of the icon of the Mother of God "The Protective Veil". Composed by Saint Innokenti (Borisov), archbishop of Kherson, in 1840.
4. Acathistos hymn in honour of the icon of the Mother of God "Smolenskaya" or "Hodigitria" (She who shows the way). The author is unknown. Composed probably in the middle of the 19th century.
5. Acathistos hymn in honour of the icon of the Mother of God "Unfading Blossom". The author is unknown. Composed probably at the beginning of the 19th century.

6. Acathistos hymn in honour of the icon of the Mother of God "The Unconsumed burning Bush". Composed by the writer A. F. Kovalevski, in 1884.
7. Acathistos hymn in honour of the icon of the Mother of God "The Joy of All Who sorrow". The author is unknown. It was published in 1913 in Nizhni Novgorod.

Let those whose heart is hardened and bitter seek the help of the Mother of God who mollifies the wicked hearts.
Let those who feel that their mind and ability to think is growing weak, or who want to study the Holy Scripture or theology, appeal to Her Who increases intelligence.
Let those who are looking for protection and security consider the miraculous vision of Saint Andrew, who could contemplate how the Mother of God spread her Protective Veil over the Christ-loving people of Constantinople.
Let those who lose the way and go off track in life look at the Virgin, who shows the Way to her Son, Who is the Eternal Truth.
Let those who in this age corrupted by sexism, seek purity of the heart as well as of the body, resort to the Unfading Blossom of virginity. Then the gates will open and they will contemplate God and Christ will turn the water of our struggle into the wine of joy.
Let those who want to protect their house against fire and burglars, or against the fire which burns in their own hearts, fire of lust or hate, seek their comfort by the Unconsumed burning Bush, the symbol of the Mother of God which was shown to Moses.
Let those who are full of sorrow or who have sad and despondent people in their families and among their friends, turn to Her Who is the Joy of all who sorrow.

So, for ourselves and for our loved ones, we may always ask the help of her who has a mother's boldness towards the Lord.

While praying, the faithful will repeatedly find in the text prayers for the Russian people or land. They may of course pray for their own country instead, or they may pray for the whole of Orthodox Christianity, or even for the entire world which is after all the Creation of the loving God.

May the Most Holy Mother of God hear the cries of distress of those who call upon her and help us to find the Way to the Kingdom and to follow it until we come to Her to glorify her Eternal Son.

Archimandrite Thomas, Hegumen of the Monastery of the Mother of God the Joy of All Who sorrow, Pervijze, Belgium
On the feast of Saint Makarios the Great

Acathistos Hymn in Honour
of the Icon of the Theotokos
"She Who mollifies the wicked Hearts"

Acathistos Hymn

Kontakion 1

To the chosen one, the Virgin Mary, who is above all the daughters of the earth, the Mother of the Son of God, Whom she gave for the salvation of the world, we call with emotion: look at our life, full of sorrows, recall all the sorrow and grief that thou hast endured, and act with us according to thy mercifulness, so that we may cry to thee: Rejoice, sorrowful Mother of God, who dost transform our sorrow into joy.

Ikos 1

The angel, who announced to the shepherds of Bethlehem the birth of the Saviour of the world, together with the multitude of the heavenly host, gave praise to God, singing: "Glory to God in the highest, and on earth peace, good will toward men"(Luke 2:14) Whilst thou, the Mother of God, homeless, as there was no place in any of the inns, gave birth to thy First-Born Son in a cave and having wrapped Him in swaddling clothes, laid Him in a manger. (Luke 2:7) Realizing the sorrow of thy heart, we cry to thee:
Rejoice, thou who hast warmed thy beloved Son with thy breath;
Rejoice, thou who hast wrapped the pre-eternal Infant in swaddling clothes;
Rejoice, thou who hast nourished the Upholder of the Universe;
Rejoice, thou who hast transformed the cave into a heaven;
Rejoice, thou who hast become the altar of the cherubim;
Rejoice, thou who hast remained Virgin while giving birth and ever after;
Rejoice, sorrowful Mother of God, who dost transform our sorrow into joy.

Kontakion 2

Having seen the pre-eternal Infant, the shepherds of Bethlehem worshipped Him, and told what the angel said to them about Him. Mary preserved all their words in her heart. (Luke 2: 17-19) After seven days according to the law of Israel, Jesus was circumcised when He was eight days old: praising thy humility and patience, Theotokos, we sing to the eternal God: "Alleluia."

Ikos 2

On the fortieth day, when the days of purification were over, Jesus' parents, having their mind established in God and observing God's law, took Him to Jerusalem, in order to place Him before the Lord and offer a sacrifice to Him as is prescribed by the Law. (Luke 2: 22-24) Therefore we cry to thee:
Rejoice, thou who hast brought the Creator of the Universe to the temple of Jerusalem in fulfilment of the law;
Rejoice, as the righteous Simeon joyfully greeted thee there;
Rejoice, only Pure and Blessed amongst women;
Rejoice, thou who hast humbly carried thy Cross, adorned with sorrows;
Rejoice, thou who hast never disobeyed God's Will;
Rejoice, thou who hast given us an example of patience and humility;
Rejoice, vessel full of the grace of the Holy Spirit;
Rejoice, sorrowful Mother of God, who dost transform our sorrow into joy.

Kontakion 3

Power from above hast strengthened thee, Mother of God, when thou didst hear the righteous Simeon saying: "This child is set for the fall and rising again of many in Israel; and for a sign which shall be spoken against; (Yea, a sword shall pierce through thine own soul also,) that the thoughts of many hearts may be revealed", (Luke 2:34-35) and great grief has pierced the Theotokos' heart and she cried out mournfully to God: "Alleluia."

Ikos 3

Wanting to murder the Infant, Herod sent his men to kill all the children in Bethlehem and its outskirts, who were two years old or less, as he learned the time of birth from the Magi. (Matthew 2: 16) And behold, as God commanded Josef through His Angel, the holy family fled to Egypt and stayed there for seven years, until Herod's death. Therefore we cry to thee with emotion:
Rejoice, thou who hast endured all the adversities of wandering;
Rejoice, as all the idols of Egypt fell, not being able to stand the strength of thy Son;
Rejoice, thou who hast lived for seven years amongst impious pagans;
Rejoice, thou who hast come to Nazareth with thy pre-eternal Infant and thy husband Carpenter;
Rejoice, thou who hast lived in poverty with the righteous Josef;
Rejoice, thou who hast been constantly working all the days of thy life;
Rejoice, sorrowful Mother of God, who dost transform our sorrow into joy.

Kontakion 4

A storm of sorrow seized the Most Pure Mother, when on the way back from Jerusalem they couldn't find the adolescent Jesus among them. Therefore they returned to Jerusalem looking for Him and after three days found Him in the temple, sitting amongst the doctors, listening to them and asking them questions. "And His Mother said unto him, Son, why hast Thou thus dealt with us? behold, Thy father and I have sought Thee sorrowing. And He said unto them, How is it that ye sought Me? Know ye not that I must be about My Father's business?" (Luke 2: 46-49) And His mother preserved all these sayings in her heart, crying to God: "Alleluia."

Ikos 4

The Mother of God heard that Jesus was going about all Galilee, teaching in the synagogues, and preaching the gospel of the kingdom, and healing all manner of sickness and all manner of disease among the people.
And His fame went throughout all Syria: and they brought unto Him all sick people that were taken with diverse diseases and torments, and those which were possessed with devils, and those which were lunatic, and those that had the palsy; and He healed them. (Matt. 4: 23 -24)
While thou, Mother of God, who knew the prophesies, hast been grieving in thy heart, foreseeing that the time will come soon, when thy Son will sacrifice Himself to atone for the sins of the world.
Therefore we praise thee, Mother of God, who suffered much, crying:
Rejoice, thou who hast given thy Son to serve the people of Israel;

Rejoice, whose heart is full of sorrow, but still obeys God's will.
Rejoice, thou who hast saved the world from another Flood;
Rejoice, thou who hast crushed the head of the ancient snake.
Rejoice, thou who hast sacrificed thyself to the living God;
Rejoice, as God is with thee, blessed one.
Rejoice, sorrowful Mother of God, who dost transform our sorrow into joy.

Kontakion 5

Preaching on earth the Kingdom of God, Jesus has unmasked the Pharisees' pride, who thought of themselves as being righteous. And when the chief priests and Pharisees had heard His parables, they perceived that He spoke of them. But when they sought to lay hands on Him, they feared the multitude, because they took him for a prophet. (Matt. 21: 45-46) Knowing all this, the Theotokos grieved about her beloved Son, being afraid that they would kill Him, and crying in her sorrow: "Alleluia."

Ikos 5

Some of the Jews, having seen the resurrection of Lazarus, went to the Pharisees, and told them what things Jesus had done.
And one of them, named Caiaphas, being the high priest that same year, said unto them: "It is expedient for us, that one man should die for the people, and that the whole nation perish not."
Then from that day forth they took counsel together how to put him to death; (John 11: 49-53) while we cry out to the most pure one:
Rejoice, thou who hast given birth to the Saviour of the world;

Rejoice, origin of our salvation.
Rejoice, thou who from thy birth hast been chosen as the Mother of our Saviour;
Rejoice, Mother of God, condemned to suffering.
Rejoice, blessed one, who hast become the Queen of Heaven;
Rejoice, thou who openly prays for us.
Rejoice, sorrowful Mother of God, who dost transform our sorrow into joy.

Kontakion 6

Judas Iscariot, one of the apostles, first a preacher of God's word, and later the betrayer, went to the chief priests to betray his Teacher; when they heard that they became very glad and promised to give him some pieces of silver. While thee, Mother of God, grieving about thy beloved Son, hast been crying to God: "Alleluia."

Ikos 6

The Last Supper dawned for Christ's disciples, when the Teacher washed their feet, giving them an example of humility, and said unto them: "One of you which eateth with Me shall betray Me." (Marc 14:18) While we, feeling compassion for the sorrow of the Mother of God, cry to her:
Rejoice, Mother of God, exhausted by the torments of thy heart;
Rejoice, thou who hast endured all the ordeals of this world, full of sorrow;
Rejoice, thou who hast found consolation in prayer;
Rejoice, the joy of all who sorrow.
Rejoice, the reliever of our grievance;
Rejoice, thou who hast saved us from the mire of sin.

Rejoice, sorrowful Mother of God, who dost transform our sorrow into joy.

Kontakion 7

Willing to reveal His love to humankind at the Last Supper, the Lord Jesus Christ took bread, and blessed it, and brake it, and gave it to the disciples, saying Take, eat; this is My body. And He took the cup, and gave thanks, and gave it to them, saying, Drink ye all of it; For this is My blood of the new testament, which is shed for many for the remission of sins." (Matt. 26: 26-28) Thanking the merciful God for His unspeakable mercifulness to us, we sing to Him: "Alleluia."

Ikos 7

The Lord revealed a new sign of His favour to His disciples, when He promised to send them the Comforter, the Spirit of Truth, which comes from the Father and will testify about Him. While to you, the Mother of God, who was sanctified twice by the Holy Spirit, we cry:
Rejoice, dwelling of the Holy Spirit;
Rejoice, all-holy mansion;
Rejoice, spacious field of the God – Word;
Rejoice, having given birth to the Divine pearl.
Rejoice, thou who hast opened for us the doors of paradise through thy Child;
Rejoice, thou through whom God's favour to us has been revealed.
Rejoice, sorrowful Mother of God, who dost transform our sorrow into joy.

Kontakion 8

It is strange and sorrowful for us to hear, how Judas Iscariot has betrayed by a kiss his Teacher and Lord; then the band and the captain and officers of the Jews took Jesus, and bound him, and led him away first to Annas; and then to Caiaphas, the high priest. While the Mother of God, foreseeing the death sentence of her beloved Son, cried to God: "Alleluia."

Ikos 8

And the whole multitude of Jews led Jesus unto Pilate, accusing Him of being a villain.
And they began to accuse him, saying, We found this man perverting the nation, and forbidding to give tribute to Caesar, saying that he himself is Christ a King. (Luke 23:2)
And after questioning Him, Pilate said to the chief priests and to the people, I find no fault in this man. (Luke 23:5)
And we cry to thee, Mother of God:
Rejoice, whose heart was tortured by grief;
Rejoice, thou who shed tears for thy beloved Son.
Rejoice, thou who endured everything without a murmur, as God's servant;
Rejoice, thou who dost grieve and sob.
Rejoice, Queen of heaven and earth, who doth receive the prayers of thy servants;
Rejoice, sorrowful Mother of God, who dost transformed our sorrow into joy.

Kontakion 9

All generations call thee blessed, more honourable than the Cherubim, and more glorious beyond compare than the Seraphim, our Lady and the Mother of our Saviour, who brought joy to the whole world by thy childbirth, and who sorrowed greatly, seeing thy beloved Son being handed over to mockery, beating and death. And we cry to thee, most pure, our song full of emotion, singing to God Almighty: "Alleluia."

Ikos 9

The most eloquent orators cannot describe all Thy suffering, our Saviour, when the soldiers made a crown of thorns and put it on Thy head and clothed Thee with purple, and saluted Thee: "Hail, King of the Jews!", and smote Thee on the head. While we, being aware of thy suffering, o Mother of God, cry to thee:
Rejoice, thou who hast seen the One Whom thou hast fed with thy milk being tortured;
Rejoice, thou who hast seen Him crowned with thorns and clothed with purple.
Rejoice, thou who hast felt His suffering;
Rejoice, thou who hast seen Him abandoned by His disciples;
Rejoice, thou who hast seen Him condemned by the unrighteous judges.
Rejoice, sorrowful Mother of God, who dost transform our sorrow into joy.

Kontakion 10

Wanting to save Jesus, Pilate said to the Jews: "But ye have a custom, that I should release unto you one at the passover: will ye therefore that I release unto you the King of the Jews?" Then cried they all again, saying, Not this man, but Barabbas. (John 18: 39-40) Praising God's mercy that He let His Only begotten Son be crucified and thus redeemed us from eternal death, we cry to Him: "Alleluia."

Ikos 10

Be for us, who have become exhausted from sorrow and illnesses, o Lady, a wall and a fence, as thou also hast suffered, hearing the Jews shouting: "Crucify Him!". Now hear us, crying to thee:
Rejoice, Mother of Mercifulness, who wipes off the tears of those who suffer cruelly;
Rejoice, thou who dost induce in us tears of emotion.
Rejoice, saviour of perishing sinners;
Rejoice, glorious intercessor of Christians.
Rejoice, thou who dost deliver us from passions;
Rejoice, thou who dost comfort the grief-stricken hearts.
Rejoice, sorrowful Mother of God, who dost transform our sorrow into joy.

Kontakion 11

Our most tender singing we bring to the Saviour of the world, Who carried His cross Himself, approaching His voluntary suffering at the crucifixion; Now there stood by the cross of Jesus His mother, and His mother's sister, Mary the wife of Cleophas, and Mary Magdalene. When Jesus therefore saw His mother, and the disciple standing by, whom He loved, He saith unto His mother, Woman, behold thy son! Then saith He to the disciple, Behold thy mother! And from that hour that disciple took her unto his own home. (John 19: 25-27) While thou, Mother of God, watching the suffering of thy Son on the cross, hast been crying grieving to God: "Alleluia."

Ikos 11

"My Light, my pre-eternal God and Creator of all creatures, how is it possible that Thou dost suffer on the cross?" The Pure Virgin said to Thee crying about Thy marvellous birth. "My Son, I was extolled above all the mothers, but now my womb is burning as I see Thee crucified."
We shed tears, listening to thy sorrow, and cry to thee:
Rejoice, thou who hast been deprived of joy and merriment;
Rejoice, thou who hast seen the voluntary suffering of thy Son on the cross.
Rejoice, thou who hast seen thy Offspring covered with wounds;
Rejoice, thou Mother-lamb, who hast seen thy Offspring being led to the slaughter like a Lamb;
Rejoice, thou who hast seen the Healer of the soul and bodily wounds covered with wounds;
Rejoice, thou who hast seen thy Son resurrected from death.
Rejoice, sorrowful Mother of God, who dost transform our sorrow into joy.

Kontakion 12

Send us Thy blessing, all-merciful Saviour, Who gave up Thy spirit on the cross and thus has torn to pieces the list of our transgressions. "Behold my good Light, my God, went out on the cross," the Virgin cried. "Try, Josef, to reach Pilate, and ask his permission to take down from the cross thy Teacher.

When I saw Thee, my Offspring, on the cross, wounded, naked and inglorious, a sword pierced my own soul also, as the righteous Simeon has prophesied," said the Mother of God, crying: "Alleluia."

Ikos 12

Praising in hymns Thy mercifulness, Lover of human kind, we worship the richness of Thy grace, Lord. "Willing to save Thy creature, Thou hast undergone death," said the most pure. "But have mercy on all of us as Thou hast risen, while we sing with emotion to Thy most pure mother:
Rejoice, thou who hast seen dead and without breath the Lord of goodness;
Rejoice, thou who hast kissed the body of thy beloved Son.
Rejoice, thou who hast seen thy Light and thy Son dead, naked and wounded;
Rejoice, thou who hast watched Him put in the grave
Rejoice, thou who hast swaddled his body with a new shroud;
Rejoice, thou who hast seen Him resurrected.
Rejoice, sorrowful Mother of God, who dost transform our sorrow into joy.

Kontakion 13

O all-praised Mother, who was exhausted from sorrow by the Cross of thy Son and God, hear our sighs and tears and deliver from sorrow, illness and eternal death, us who put our trust in thy unspeakable mercifulness and cry to God "Alleluia."
(This Kontakion is read three times, then Ikos 1 and Kontakion 1 should be read.)

Prayer to the most holy Theotokos before her icon "She who mollifies the wicked hearts"

O sorrowful Mother of God, who art above all the daughters of the earth according to thy purity and the great suffering that thou hast endured on earth, accept our grieving and preserve us under the veil of thy grace. As we do not have another shelter and warm intercessor but thee, and as thou hast boldness towards the One, Who was born from thee, help us and save us by thy prayers, so that without obstacles we may reach the Kingdom of Heaven, where, together with all the saints, we will praise the One Triune God, now and forever and unto the ages of ages.

Troparion, tone 5

Mollify our wicked hearts, o Theotokos, and turn away the attacks of those who hate us, and deliver our souls from every distress as looking at Thy holy image we feel moved by Thy mercifulness towards us and we kiss thy wounds; the pain we cause thee by our arrows, horrifies us. Don't let us, o good Mother, perish in our hardheartedness and because of the hardheartedness of our neighbours, as thou canst truly mollify the wicked hearts.

Acathistos Hymn in Honour
of the Icon of the Theotokos
"The Increase of Intelligence"

Kontakion 1

To the Mother of God, the one chosen out of all generations, the Queen of Heaven and earth, who grants a spiritual cure to the entire world, we offer a hymn of gratefulness after receiving the Divine treasure, her miracle working icon "The Increase of Intelligence". Being guarded by it, we feel a light joy and call lovingly: Rejoice, all-merciful Lady, who dost grant wisdom and reason to thy faithful people.

Ikos 1

The angel-herald has been sent to the city of Nazareth to the pure maiden Mary to say to her: "Rejoice", when God the Word was incarnated in her womb. Having heard the Annunciation, the most pure Virgin spake out of the humility of her heart: "Behold the handmaid of the Lord; be it unto me according to Thy word" (Luke 1:38).
While we, the sinners, reverently honouring the Mother of Christ our God and having learned from the Archangel, cry out with emotion:
Rejoice, thou who art blessed among women. (Luke 1: 28)
Rejoice, thou who art favoured by God.
Rejoice, thou who art shielded by God's strength.
Rejoice, thou who art sanctified by the Holy Ghost.
Rejoice, thou who art God's faithful handmaid.
Rejoice, thou who art chosen by God.
Rejoice, thou who hast given birth to the Saviour of the world.
Rejoice, thou Mother of the Light, which illuminates all.
Rejoice, thou who dost excel the wisdom of the sages;
Rejoice, thou who dost give reason to thy faithful ones.
Rejoice, Queen of Heaven and earth;
Rejoice, for all generations shall call thee blessed. (Luke 1: 48)

Rejoice, all-merciful Lady who dost grant wisdom and reason to thy faithful people.

Kontakion 2

Knowing the wish, o most pure, of the newly enlightened ones, thou hast blessed the herald of the Gospel's mysteries, the apostle Luke, to paint an image of thy most pure countenance. Looking at this image, thou hast said imperiously: "My Grace and my strength will be with this image." Therefore reverently honouring thy holy icons, with which thou hast adorned the entire Christian world, we cry to God thanking Him for thee: "Alleluia."

Ikos 2

Opening for us the heavenly reason, most pure Virgin, thou dost let all thy faithful learn about God's will, which is good, pleasing and perfect, and excels all reason. Take care of us, all-praised Theotokos, give us the light of truth, comfort us like a Mother, teach us the path of truth, so that we may cry to thee praying:
Rejoice, thou who hast given birth to Christ, God's Strength and Wisdom.
Rejoice, thou who hast united God and Man.
Rejoice, thou who hast enlightened our souls with the light of reason.
Rejoice, thou who hast held the unspeakable glory of God.
Rejoice, thou who dost sanctify the honour given to the holy icons.
Rejoice, giver of spiritual treasures.
Rejoice, thou who hast granted Grace to thy glorious icons.
Rejoice, as gazing at thy icons we worship thee.

Rejoice, thou who through thy holy icons dost heal in the whole world.
Rejoice, thou who dost lift up our minds and hearts to heaven.
Rejoice, thou who hast illuminated the entire universe by the rays of thy Grace.
Rejoice, thou who dost reign eternally together with thy Son and God.
Rejoice, all-merciful Lady who dost grant wisdom and reason to thy faithful people.

Kontakion 3

Being shielded by the power of God's Grace, pious people came to the city of Nazareth and found there the Theotokos' house, where the most pure Virgin was born and received the Annunciation. They moved that house to Italy, to the city of Loreto. There, on the top of the house, is an icon of the Mother of God, painted on wood; invisible angel forces surround it and praise it magnificently, singing joyfully to God: "Alleluia."

Ikos 3

Having the mercifulness of a mother for Christians, Most Pure, thou dost call all lands on earth to salvation. Therefore people of various nationalities visit thy house and confess their sins before thine icon. And the glory of thine icon dost shine in East and West, and people delivered from sicknesses, sorrows and misfortunes give thee thanks, crying:
Rejoice, House, created by God's Wisdom for Himself.
Rejoice, City of God, which originated from the small city of Nazareth.
Rejoice, thou who hast sanctified the house of God by thy Presentation.
Rejoice, thou who art greater than the Holy of the Holiest.

Rejoice, thou who hast come to Nazareth with the pre-eternal Infant.
Rejoice, thou who hast served the mystery of salvation of mankind.
Rejoice, thou who art the ladder by which we ascend from earth to Heaven.
Rejoice, miraculous protective veil for the whole world.
Rejoice, for we honour faithfully the image of thy most pure countenance.
Rejoice, for we receive from thee the blessed gifts for our salvation.
Rejoice, thou who dost manifest miraculous signs through thine icons.
Rejoice, thou who art the powerful Protector of Christians.
Rejoice, all-merciful Lady who dost grant wisdom and reason to thy faithful people.

Kontakion 4

The storm of sorrow had seized a painter, whose reason was darkened and who couldn't find help from earthly physicians. Then the most pure Mother of God appeared to him and commanded him to paint her icon, which now sanctifies her house in Loreto. Having done this, the painter was healed and from that time on he called the newly painted icon "The Increase of Intelligence", singing before it God's praise: "Alleluia."

Ikos 4

When the people of Russia came to know that the most holy Theotokos gave them, for their joy and consolation, her icon, called "the Increase of Intelligence", they adorned their temples and houses with many copies of it. Many wondrous signs and miracles happen through these copies for those who faithfully come to them and sing to the most blessed one:

Rejoice, thou who hast granted us thy glorious image to sanctify and comfort us.

Rejoice, thou who dost quickly cure bodily and spiritual illnesses.

Rejoice, thou who hast shielded the Russian land with the veil of thy favour;

Rejoice, thou who hast delivered those who love and honour thy image, from all misfortunes.

Rejoice, thou who dost enter invisibly our houses through thy Graceful icon.

Rejoice, thou who dost bring us blessing and joy.

Rejoice, thou who dost take in thy all-mighty hands those abandoned by physicians.

Rejoice, thou who dost heal those who lost their mind through illness.

Rejoice, hope of the hopeless.

Rejoice, enlightener of our minds.

Rejoice, pure mirror which reflects the truth.

Rejoice, thou whose name is praised in East and West.

Rejoice, all-merciful Lady who dost grant wisdom and reason to thy faithful people.

Kontakion 5

Thy icon, Theotokos, has appeared as a Divine star, for it sanctifies our country and its cities, it enlightens those darkened by ignorance with the light of theology, it illuminates our reason, darkened by sins, it sets the lost on the path following the commandments of thy Son and God, and we cry to Him thankfully: "Alleluia."

Ikos 5

Having seen the Divine treasure, the wondrous icon of the Mother of God, we pray to her diligently, finding there the cure of our ailments, relief of our sorrows, salvation from our misfortunes and we sing joyfully to our Lady-Protector:

Rejoice, thou who hast enlightened the faithful by the appearance of thine icon.

Rejoice, thou through whom the Sun of Truth, Christ, our God, started to shine in the darkness.

Rejoice, mother of the Light of Reason, that enlightened by its Grace the whole universe.

Rejoice, thou who dost enlighten us by thy blessing.

Rejoice, thou who dost dispel the gloom of our ignorance by thy light.

Rejoice, Virgin, for through thee the light of theology started to shine for all.

Rejoice, inextinguishable candle, which kindles the light of faith.

Rejoice, thou who dost illuminate the path of virtue.

Rejoice, thou who art the source of all that is sacred;

Rejoice, thou who dost guard us powerfully from adversities and misfortunes.

Rejoice, inextinguishable light of Divine love.

Rejoice, thou who dost proclaim to us the spring of salvation by the light of thy miracles.

Rejoice, all-merciful Lady who dost grant wisdom and reason to thy faithful people.

Kontakion 6

Thy favours are known in the entire world, Mother of our Lord, for in many cities and villages of the Russian land thy icon "The Increase of Intelligence" shines with the rays of miracles, enlightening our souls by the light of God's Grace and prompting us to sing to God, Who honoured thee: "Alleluia."

Ikos 6

There appeared the light of salvation in thy glorious icon, Theotokos, for all who stray in the darkness of sins and passions, and swift help is rendered to all those who pray before it faithfully and reverently. Remove the darkness from our minds, o all-praised, by thy light and show the True Light to all who cry to thee lovingly:
Rejoice, inextinguishable star, that hast given to the world the Sun of Truth;
Rejoice, thou Mother of True Light, which enlightens the souls of the faithful.
Rejoice, mentor of the blessed teaching.
Rejoice, thou who dost shield our darkened mind with a light veil.
Rejoice, thou who art the dawn which dispels the haze of our sins.
Rejoice, thou who dost deliver us from darkness and eternal torment.
Rejoice, thou who dost free us from the enemy's nets;
Rejoice, thou who dost win a victory over the madness of the world.
Rejoice, thou who dost expel teachings, harmful for the soul;
Rejoice, thou who art the giver of knowledge useful for the soul.

Rejoice, thou who dost comfort us with thy icon.
Rejoice, thou who encourages the souls with the light of joy.
Rejoice, all-merciful Lady who dost grant wisdom and reason to thy faithful people.

Kontakion 7

Willing all men to be saved and to realize the truth, our most merciful Lord and Creator has granted us the image of His most pure Mother, called "The Increase of Intelligence", so that those praying before it, having received strength in using word, reason and wisdom, sing, free from wandering thoughts, to our King and God: "Alleluia."

Ikos 7

Mother of God, thou who dost manifest new and even more glorious wonders through thy holy icon: by the power of Christ's Grace thou dost enlighten those with darkened minds, deter men from madness, strengthen the weak, and promptly help all who turn to thy healing image, inspiring them to sing to thee:
Rejoice, thou who dost pull us out of the depth of ignorance.
Rejoice, thou who dost enlighten the minds of many.
Rejoice, thou who dost grant wise words to those who ask.
Rejoice, thou who dost make fools reason clearly.
Rejoice, thou who dost drive away sinful designs.
Rejoice, thou who dost soften embittered hearts.
Rejoice, thou who dost elevate the mind to God;
Rejoice, thou who dost make the unwise wise.
Rejoice, thou who dost encourage us to strive for piety.
Rejoice, thou who dost clothe us with eternal joy.
Rejoice, thou who dost bring the prayers of the faithful to thy Son and God.

Rejoice, thou who dost pray incessantly before the Throne of the Almighty for us all.
Rejoice, all-merciful Lady who dost grant wisdom and reason to thy faithful people.

Kontakion 8

It is amazing to see, how thine icon, o most pure Theotokos, painted on a piece of wood, drives away the spirits of darkness by thy Divine power and gives reason to those seized by feebleness of mind and by trouble in learning. Therefore we, perishing because of our sins, plead with thee tearfully: deliver us from our visible and invisible enemies, from the darkness of ignorance, so that we may always sing to our Saviour and God: "Alleluia."

Ikos 8

The whole of the Russian land has an abundance of thy miracle working icons, o Virgin Theotokos, that shine like God's bright stars. Amongst them also the Grace of thy icon "The Increase of intelligence" shines and warms our frozen hearts by the signs of thy favour to us, sinners. Therefore, kneeling before thy holy countenance, we praise thee, our most pure Mother:
Rejoice, thou who dost transform our sorrows into joy;
Rejoice, thou who dost defend us from the burning arrows of the Evil One.
Rejoice, thou who dost bring up children and shield them with thy Grace.
Rejoice, thou who art the wise Protector and Mentor of the young.
Rejoice, thou who dost grant reason to children that are poor learners.

Rejoice, thou who dost destroy the traps of the enemy.
Rejoice, thou who dost enlighten the mind of the faithful.
Rejoice, thou who dost disgrace the unfaithful.
Rejoice, thou who dost heal those seized by madness;
Rejoice, thou whose blissful icon drives away the demons;
Rejoice, Mother of mercifulness and generosity;
Rejoice, hope of our salvation.
Rejoice, all-merciful Lady who dost grant wisdom and reason to thy faithful people.

Kontakion 9

All the angels serve thee reverently, Queen of Heaven and earth, while mankind praises thee and honours thy holy icon that thou hast granted to comfort and rejoice us. Teach us, o most good Lady, to praise thee worthily and to sing to the Saviour of the world, who was born from thee "Alleluia."

Ikos 9

The eloquent orators of humankind can neither grasp the mystery of thy service to Christians nor can they explain the miraculous power of thine icons which benefits in every way the soul and the body of man. While we, orthodox, standing with tears of joy before thine holy icons, praise thee, o Grace giving one, and say:
Rejoice, thou who art the joy of the Angels;
Rejoice, thou who art worshipped by Archangels.
Rejoice, thou whom the Cherubim receive in the air.
Rejoice, thou who art praised by the Seraphim.
Rejoice, bright adornment of both the churches of heaven and earth.
Rejoice, thou who art above all the powers of the heavens.
Rejoice, thou who art honoured by the host of the heavens;

Rejoice, thou who art the glory of all who live on earth.
Rejoice, thou who dost elevate our minds to the Highest by thy example;
Rejoice, our guide to our fatherland in the heavens.
Rejoice, thou who dost enlighten the whole earth by the radiance of thy soul;
Rejoice, thou who hast adopted us all at the Cross of thy Son.
Rejoice, all-merciful Lady who dost grant wisdom and reason to thy faithful people.

Kontakion 10

Having wished to save the world from insanity and the enemy's delusions, the Lord, the lover of mankind, has granted us thy wondrous icon, o Mother of God. Praying before it the insane are cured, the possessed are freed from demons, the sorrowful find joy and comfort. Praising God, Who is so merciful to us, we cry to Him gratefully: "Alleluia."

Ikos 10

Be for us an unbreakable wall and a protective veil, all-pure Mother of God, against the armies of visible and invisible enemies; guard us from misfortunes and diseases. Therefore kneeling before thy icon "The Increase of Intelligence", and firmly believing in thy blissful help and cure of all spiritual and bodily illnesses, we cry joyfully to thee:
Rejoice, thou who dost deter us from the ways of perdition.
Rejoice, thou who dost guide the faithful on the path of truth.
Rejoice, thou who dost drive away the spirit of sickness and despondency;
Rejoice, thou who dost help obtain the spirit of reason and strength.
Rejoice, thou who dost disgrace the enemies by God's might.

Rejoice, thou who dost bring to ruin impious assemblies.
Rejoice, cure of the possessed.
Rejoice, thou who dost heal all aggressive diseases.
Rejoice, thou who dost deliver us from spiritual death.
Rejoice, thou who dost wash away our sins with thy tears.
Rejoice, thou who dost satiate us miraculously with spiritual joy;
Rejoice, thou who dost grant us eternal joy also in the ages to come.
Rejoice, all-merciful Lady who dost grant wisdom and reason to thy faithful people.

Kontakion 11

We sing thankfully before thy most pure image, o most pure, for thy unspeakable mercifulness, and we pray to thee who art full of Divine Grace: guard our minds and hearts against pernicious teachings, disbelief and superstitions; keep our land free from all kinds of disorders, which are stirred up by the enemies of faith, and let us praise our Creator with a pure heart, singing: "Alleluia."

Ikos 11

We see thine icon, o Theotokos, like a burning candle, which enlightens our land with the light of thy miracles, sets us on the path of salvation and kindles our hearts with love for thee, most pure Mother of our God. Therefore, knowing the power of thy Grace, we glorify thee with hymns of joy:
Rejoice, thou whose wisdom is immeasurably higher than the wisdom of Solomon;
Rejoice, thou who dost reveal God's most secret mysteries to thy faithful.

Rejoice, thou who dost transform the dull-witted into lovers of wisdom;
Rejoice, thou who art a light which enlightens our souls.
Rejoice, thou who dost disgrace the vain wisdom of this age.
Rejoice, thou who dost set on the right path those blinded by vain wisdom.
Rejoice, thou who dost renew the mind of those who pray sincerely;
Rejoice, thou who dost place a happy thought in the heart at the time of confusion.
Rejoice, thou who art the revelation of God's Wisdom and Goodness;
Rejoice, thou who art the beauty of the heavens.
Rejoice, thou who hast given us a heavenly gift, thy miracle working icon.
Rejoice, source of incessant joy.
Rejoice, all-merciful Lady who dost grant wisdom and reason to thy faithful people.

Kontakion 12

Obtain for us the Divine Grace from thy Son and God, o all-good one; hold out thy helping hand to us, that we do not perish without repentance; shield us with thy love; cleanse our minds of sinful designs; clear the eyes of our heart that we may see the path of salvation and grant us to sing to our Creator and God in this life and in the Kingdom of Heaven: "Alleluia."

Ikos 12

Singing the miracles, which have been manifested through thine icon, o Lady, we praise, glorify and honour thee who art more honourable than the Cherubim, and more glorious beyond compare than the Seraphim. Look at us, standing before thy holy icon, Theotokos, who art now in the heavens, and send us thy blessing; deliver us from all misfortune and the enemy's temptations, for we honour thee with songs as our Protector and Keeper:

Rejoice, thou who dost save the entire Universe with thy prayers.

Rejoice, thou who art the comfort of this sorrowful age.

Rejoice, Mother of Light, who dost enlighten everyone with the light of thy purity.

Rejoice, thou who dost reveal to us the mysteries of God's will.

Rejoice, thou who hast chosen Russia as thy lot and thy domain.

Rejoice, thou who hast blessed this land by thy miracle working icons.

Rejoice, thou who dost elevate us to the Light of Truth through thine image;

Rejoice, thou who dost shield us invisibly with its Divine Grace.

Rejoice, thou who dost pour blessed joy into God-loving hearts.

Rejoice, thou who dost open the doors of God's mercy by thine entreaty.

Rejoice, thou who dost help us to court the gifts of the Holy Ghost;

Rejoice, thou who art the only pure and blessed amongst women.

Rejoice, all-merciful Lady who dost grant wisdom and reason to thy faithful people.

Kontakion 13

O all-praised Mother of the pre-eternal Light and Wisdom of the Father, thou art the light of the darkened, the increase of intelligence and the joy of our hearts; hear and accept the pleading of us, sinners; make us, who are unwise, wiser and teach us to sing and pray before thine icon, called "The increase of Intelligence". Do not stop praying for us, thine unworthy servants, who glorify thee and sing to thy Son and God: "Alleluia."
(This Kontakion is read three times, then Ikos 1 and Kontakion 1 should be read.)

Prayers to the most holy Theotokos before her icon "The Increase of Intelligence"

First Prayer

O most holy Virgin, thou art the Bride of God the Father and the Mother of His Divine Son Jesus Christ! Thou art the Queen of Angels and the salvation of mankind, thou dost unmask sinners and punish apostates. Have mercy upon us, who have sinned heavily and not fulfilled God's commandments; who have broken the vows of baptism and of monasticism and many other vows that we have promised to keep.

When the Holy Ghost abandoned King Saul, fear and depression seized him and the darkness of despair and a joyless soul tortured him. And now we also, because of our sins, are deprived of the Grace of the Holy Spirit. Our mind is corrupted by idle thoughts, our soul is darkened since we have forgotten God, and now our hearts are crowded with all kinds of sorrows, grievances, illnesses, hatred, malice, hostility, vindictiveness, pleasure at another's misfortune, and other sins. And, having no joy or consolation, we call to thee, the Mother of our God Jesus Christ, to move thy Son by thine entreaties to forgive us our transgressions and to send us the Spirit the Comforter, as He sent Him to the apostles so that we, being comforted and enlightened by Him, would sing to thee the song of gratefulness: rejoice, most holy Theotokos who hast increased our intelligence so that we may find our salvation. Amen.

Second Prayer

My good Queen, my holy Hope, shelter of the lost and the protector of strangers, the helper of the poor and the protective veil of those in temptations, see my misfortune, see my sorrow: I am surrounded by temptations and there is no one to guard me against them. Therefore help me, as I am feeble, guide me as I am a stranger; instruct me as I have strayed; heal me and save me as I am hopeless. I have no other help, no other hope, besides thee, my Lady: help us, as we have placed our hope in thee and we glorify thee constantly, as we are thy servants, don't let us be disgraced. I kneel before thy mercy, Theotokos Virgin, do not reject my entreaties as I am full of sorrows, but deliver me from my misfortunes, as thou only art pure and blessed. Amen.

Third Prayer

O most pure Theotokos, the House that God's Wisdom has created for Himself, Giver of spiritual gifts, who dost elevate our minds from the world to the spiritual spheres and teach us reason! Accept the prayerful singing of thine unworthy servants, who worship thee with faith and emotion before thy most pure image. Entreat thy Son and our God that He may grant our authorities wisdom and power, our judges truth and justice, our pastors spiritual wisdom, zeal and vigilant guarding of our souls, our mentors humble wisdom, our children obedience, and to all of us the spirit of reason and piety, the spirit of humility and meekness, the spirit of purity and truth.
And now, o our all-praised and all-loved Mother, increase our intelligence, pacify and unite those in hostility and separation, and give them an unbreakable bond of love; direct all those who have strayed through lack of reason, to the light of Christ's truth and edify them in fear of God, abstention and love of work; give words of wisdom and knowledge, useful for the souls of those pleading with thee, who art brighter than the Cherubim and more honourable than the Seraphim. While we, seeing God's glorious works and His unfathomable

wisdom, in the world and in our lives, shall abandon all earthly vanity and excessive earthly concerns and shall elevate our minds and our hearts to the Heavens, and with thy protection and help shall glorify, thank and praise God, One in three and Creator of all, now and always and unto the ages of ages. Amen

Troparion, tone 4

O most glorious Mother of Christ, our God, who is the Giver of all good, preserve the Universe by thy mercy; give us, thy servants, wisdom and reason; enlighten our souls with the light of thy Son, thou the only all-praised, who art glorified by the Cherubim and the Seraphim.

Kontakion, tone 2

As thou dost enlighten us by the reason of the One God, we praise thee, the most pure Mother of the Reason which upholds the entire Universe. Thou art the Beauty of the visible and the invisible world and dost enlighten us by rays of life.

Acathistos Hymn in Honour
of the Icon of the Theotokos
"The Protective Veil"

Kontakion 1

O Chosen by the pre-eternal God, Queen of heaven and earth, higher than all creation, who hast in days past entered whilst praying into the Church of the Blachernae we, offering thee with thanksgiving due veneration, resort with faith and compunction under thy shining omoforion for we lie in darkness. And thou who hast invincible power dost set us free from every affliction so that we may cry to thee:
Rejoice, our Joy, protect us from every ill by thy precious Veil.

Ikos 1

Archangels and angels with John the Forerunner, John the Theologian and the choir of all the saints, were present with thee, their Queen, in the Church of the Blachernae and hearing thy moving entreaties for all the world, they cried out with wonder:
Rejoice, O pre-eternal good will of God the Father Who has no beginning of days;
Rejoice, most pure who contained the timeless God the Son.
Rejoice, thou who art the chosen dwelling-place of God the all-holy Spirit;
Rejoice, thou who art the never-ceasing wonder of the angelic hosts on high.
Rejoice, thou all-threatening terror of the dark forces of hell;
Rejoice, thou whom the many-eyed cherubim meet in the air.
Rejoice, thou to whom the six-winged seraphim sing praises;
Rejoice, thou whose most precious veil we born on earth venerate gratefully.
Rejoice, our Joy, protect us from every ill by thy precious Veil.

Kontakion 2

Saint Andrew with Epiphanios having seen thee in the air inside the Church, praying God for all Christians, recognised thee to be the Mother of Christ our God Who ascended to heaven, and prostrating themselves on the ground they joyfully venerated thine all-precious veil, crying: "Alleluia."

Ikos 2

Thou, O Theotokos Virgin art an incomprehensible defender of Orthodox people. Therefore our enemies will never know how powerful is the prayer of the Mother of God: while we being well aware of thine all-mighty protection cry to thee with tender feeling:
Rejoice, most merciful Comforter of all the afflicted and heavy laden;
Rejoice, never sleeping Guide of all those who have strayed and gone blind.
Rejoice, thou who by thy entreaties dost swiftly appease the wrath of God rightly poured out on us;
Rejoice, thou who by an all-powerful behest dost tame our evil passions.
Rejoice, thou who art the strong awakener of sleeping consciences;
Rejoice, thou who dost provide an easy overcoming of sinful practices.
Rejoice, thou owing to whom hell groans and the spirits of evil tremble;
Rejoice, thou for whose sake the gates of paradise are opened to us all.
Rejoice, our Joy, protect us from every ill by thy precious Veil.

Kontakion 3

Power from on high shields those who turn faithfully and reverently to thine all-honoured veil, seeking refuge: for to thee alone, O most holy and most pure Mother of God is it given that every petition of thine be fulfilled. Therefore the faithful of all ages glorify thee and thy Son, crying: "Alleluia."

Ikos 3

O Lady, having a never-failing wealth of mercy, thou dost stretch thy helping hand to all the ends of the earth: thou dost give healing to the sick, relief to the suffering, sight to the blind, and to all and everything what is expedient for them as they cry aloud gratefully:
Rejoice, indestructible fortress and bulwark of the Orthodox faith;
Rejoice, foremost adornment of holy churches and altars.
Rejoice, most safe guard of piety;
Rejoice, vigilant Helper of stout-hearted city governors.
Rejoice, unconquerable Head of Christian leaders and armies;
Rejoice, holy mirror of justice for incorruptible judges.
Rejoice, perfect Reason that admonishes mentors and tutors;
Rejoice, Blessing of pious houses and families.
Rejoice, our Joy, protect us from every ill by thy precious Veil.

Kontakion 4

O Lady, thou dost help us, who are seized by the storm of many afflictions: for thou dost stand before the altar of the Lord, with thy hands raised and pray that the Lord, the King of Glory would hear our unworthy prayer and be benevolent to the petitions of those who call upon thy holy Name crying to thy Son: "Alleluia."

Ikos 4

The Lord God listened to the prayers of Joshua, son of Nun, and commanded the sun to stand still until he took vengeance on his enemy, and the Lord Jesus now listens to thy entreaties, O chosen Palace of the Holy Spirit. Therefore we sinners, laying our hope in thy protection, make bold to say to thee, as thou art the Mother of God:
Rejoice, thou who art illumined by the mental Sun and who dost enlighten us with the light that never sets;
Rejoice, thou who hast illumined the whole earth by the brightness of thy most pure soul.
Rejoice, thou who hast gladdened all the heavens by the purity of thy body;
Rejoice, Protector and Provider of holy Christian monasteries.
Rejoice, thou who dost give vigour and understanding to the pastors of the Church;
Rejoice, Mentor of God-fearing monks and nuns.
Rejoice, undisturbed peace of the pious elderly.
Rejoice, secret joy of pure virgins and widows.
Rejoice, our Joy, protect us from every ill by thy precious Veil.

Kontakion 5

When Moses the God-seer, in the battle against Amalek, stood with arms uplifted, Israel prevailed; and when he let his arms fall, Amalek was victorious; strengthened by his followers, who held his arms, he defeated the enemy. While thou, O Mother of God, having raised thy hands in thine entreaty, even though no man supports them, dost always conquer the enemies of Christ: thou art an invincible shield for us who cry: "Alleluia."

Ikos 5

Having seen thee in the air inside the church of the Blachernae holding out thy hands in prayer to thy Son and God, the assemblies of saints, together with the archangels and angels sang joyfully in thanksgiving to thee. While we, being strengthened by thy hands, that are stronger than the hands of Moses, cry with emotion:
Rejoice, thou whose love and mercy towards us alone hold up thy hands for us;
Rejoice, thou whom our visible and invisible enemies cannot withstand.
Rejoice, thou who dost drive away the dark hordes of our passions and lusts;
Rejoice, thou who dost hold in thy hand the divine fire of Christ without being scorched, and with it dost set us, who are cold, aflame.
Rejoice, thou who dost crown with a fair crown of chastity those who fight against the flesh;
Rejoice, thou who art an everlasting Speaker with those who strive in fasting and silent prayer.
Rejoice, prompt Comforter of those who are exhausted by despair and sadness.
Rejoice, thou who dost provide us with blessed humility and patience.
Rejoice, our Joy, protect us from every ill by thy precious Veil.

Kontakion 6

Saint Romanos the Melodion, appeared as an advocate of thine inexhaustible grace and favour when he had received from thee in a dream a paper roll to swallow: having become wise by this, he began to sing skilfully in thy honour and to write praises for the saints, calling out with faith: "Alleluia."

Ikos 6

O Virgin, Maid of God, thou hast shone forth like the Dawn of the true Sun of righteousness, enlightening all by the wisdom of thy God and Son and who dost lead to knowledge of the truth all those who cry to thee:

Rejoice, thou who hast given birth to Christ, God's Power and God's Wisdom;

Rejoice, thou who hast put to shame the foolish wisdom of this world, and who hast set those blinded by it on the right path.

Rejoice, Keeper of our holy faith and teacher of Orthodox dogma;

Rejoice, Eradicator of impious heresies and schisms.

Rejoice, thou who dost well know what is hidden and what cannot be foreseen and dost tell it to whom it is proper;

Rejoice, thou who dost put to shame false seers and vain divinations.

Rejoice, thou who in the hour of perplexity dost plant a happy thought in our hearts;

Rejoice, thou who dost deter us from perilous undertakings and senseless desires.

Rejoice, our Joy, protect us from every ill by thy precious Veil.

Kontakion 7

The all-knowing and all-patient Lord, wishing to manifest the boundless plenty of His love and favour for mankind, has chosen thee alone to be His Mother, and made thee an invincible defence for His people: that even though one of them would appear deserving of condemnation by the righteous judgement of God, yet all the more shall he be preserved for repentance under thy mighty protection, crying: "Alleluia."

Ikos 7

O Lord, thou hast shown in thine all-pure Mother, how wonderful are thy works when her most marvellous veil appeared in her hands shining brighter than the rays of the sun and with it she protected the people in the Church of the Blachernae. Hearing of such a sign of her merciful intercession, seized by fear and joy, all say:
Rejoice, thou who hast spread thy veil, not made by the hand of man, over the whole world like a cloud;
Rejoice, thou who dost hold in thy hands the Sign of thy miraculous Son, the pre-eternal High Priest,
Rejoice, thou who hast thereby made manifest a new favour and a new grace in the Orthodox Church;
Rejoice, pillar of cloud who dost protect us all from the temptations and seductions of the world.
Rejoice, pillar of fire, which shows us all the path of salvation amidst the haze of sin;
Rejoice, thou who dost openly strengthen the known zealots of piety.
Rejoice, secret Giver of understanding to the secret servants of God in this world;
Rejoice, thou who also dost not leave me who did no good work of virtue, without thy grace and protection.
Rejoice, our Joy, protect us from every ill by thy precious Veil.

Kontakion 8

The angels praised thee, who wondrously didst appear from heaven in the Church of the Blachernae; apostles gave thee glory; the choir of holy fathers, saints and holy women lauded thee. The Forerunner with John the Theologian venerated thee, while people present in the church cried aloud with joy: "Alleluia."

Ikos 8

The Lord Who reigns over all things above and below, when He had seen thee, His Mother, standing in the Church and praying with tender feeling to Him, said: Ask, O my Mother, for I shall never turn away from thee but will fulfil all thy petitions and teach all to sing to thee in thanksgiving:
Rejoice, Ark of the Testament in which the sanctification of mankind is kept;
Rejoice, all-holy Jar in which the Bread of Eternal Life is preserved for those who do hunger for righteousness.
Rejoice, all-golden Vessel in which the flesh and blood of the divine Lamb are prepared for us;
Rejoice, thou who dost receive in thine all-powerful arms those forsaken by the physicians.
Rejoice, thou who dost raise from their sick-bed those crippled bodily but not in spirit and faith;
Rejoice, thou who dost give a new and better understanding to those who are perishing from a diseased mind.
Rejoice, thou who dost wisely make us trip on the smooth path of sin and passion;
Rejoice, thou who dost mollify the cruelty of our unrepentant heart.
Rejoice, our Joy, protect us from every ill by thy precious Veil.

Kontakion 9

The entire assembly of angels offers praises to thee, the true Mother of God and Defender of all who resort to thee, knowing how with thine unfailing protection thou dost gladden the righteous, plead for the sinners, protect and deliver the poor, and pray for all the faithful crying: "Alleluia."

Ikos 9

The verbose orators are at a loss, like dumb fish, as to how to praise as is due, the great feast of thine all-precious protection: for all the things said by them about thee suffice not to number all thy favours. While we, seeing thine innumerable good deeds, cry with joy:
Rejoice, thou who dost guard us from the deadly plague in which all perish;
Rejoice, thou who dost preserve cities and villages from sudden earthquakes.
Rejoice, thou who dost lead us with thy strong arm away from flood and drowning;
Rejoice, thou who dost protect us from fire by the dew of thy prayers.
Rejoice, thou who dost provide us with the Bread of Life and save us from hunger of soul and body;
Rejoice, thou who dost turn away from our heads the blows of lightning and thunder.
Rejoice, thou who dost guard us against the invasions of strange peoples and disguised assassins;
Rejoice, thou who dost guard us by peace and love against family quarrels and the enmities of those of our blood.
Rejoice, our Joy, protect us from every ill by thy precious Veil.

Kontakion 10

Wishing to save mankind from the enemy's delusions, the mankind-loving Lord gave us on earth, thee, His Mother, to be our help, protection and defence, to be the Comforter of those that sorrow, the Joy of the afflicted, the Defender of the aggrieved, and to raise from the depth of sin all those who sing: "Alleluia."

Ikos 10

"O King of Heaven," spoke the all-pure Queen in prayer as She stood in the air with the angels, "do accept every man praying to Thee and calling upon my name for help, so that he would not leave my assembly with nothing and unheard." Hearing this most good prayer, the assemblies of the saints cried in thanksgiving:
Rejoice, thou who dost crown the husbandmen who are pure of hand and heart with blessed fruits;
Rejoice, Succour and righteous Reward of all those who trade honestly.
Rejoice, thou who dost reprove publicly those who keep not their oaths and whose gains are unjust;
Rejoice, unexpected Helper of those in distress in their travels by land and water.
Rejoice, thou who dost gladden the childless couples with the fruits of faith and the spirit;
Rejoice, invisible Tutor of motherless orphans.
Rejoice, strong Defender of those in captivity and exile.
Rejoice, ever-watchful Guardian of those sitting in bonds and prisons.
Rejoice, our Joy, protect us from every ill by thy precious Veil.

Kontakion 11

Listening to tender singing and hearing thy prayer for us, we beg thee, O Virgin Theotokos, do not neglect the petitions of thy servants for we resort to thee when assaulted and afflicted, and in our distress we pour out our tears before thee, crying: "Alleluia."

Ikos 11

Seeing thee in the air burning in prayer like a candle, the Blachernae Church itself exclaimed together with the multitude of people present there: "And whence is this to me, that the mother of my Lord should come to me?" (Luke 1:43) And Saint Andrew with Epiphanios prayed warmly to thee, crying:
Rejoice, generous Giver of all spiritual and bodily gifts;
Rejoice, true Advocate of sinners who have started to repent.
Rejoice, wont Champion of those struggling with the passions and the enemy's wicked additions; Rejoice, invisible Tamer of cruel and bestial rulers.
Rejoice, secret Rest and Consolation of humble and suffering servants;
Rejoice, longed-for Fulfiller of blessed marriages.
Rejoice, swift and painless relief of mothers in childbirth;
Rejoice, our only Help in the hour of death.
Rejoice, our Joy, protect us from every ill by thy precious Veil.

Kontakion 12

Ask the Divine grace for us from thy Son; hold out to us thy helping hand; ward off from us every enemy and adversary and pacify our lives so that we perish not cruelly and without repentance, but accept us, O our Protector, in thy eternal mansions, that, rejoicing, we may cry to thee: "Alleluia."

Ikos 12

Singing of thy mighty protection, we glorify thee as our firm Advocate and we venerate thee who dost pray for us: for we believe and we trust that thou wilt beg of thy Son and God eternal and temporal good things for all who cry lovingly to thee thus:

Rejoice, strong Defence of the whole inhabited earth;
Rejoice, sanctification of all the earthly and heavenly elements.
Rejoice, Blessing of all the seasons of the year;
Rejoice, thou who dost ward off all assaults and temptations that come from the world, the flesh and the devil.
Rejoice, unexpected Reconciliation of those who are in bitter enmity;
Rejoice, Amendment without their knowledge of unrepentant sinners.
Rejoice, thou who dost not turn away from those despised and rejected by all;
Rejoice, thou who dost pluck from the edge of the pit of destruction those that indeed despair.
Rejoice, our Joy, protect us from every ill by thy precious Veil.

Kontakion 13

O all-praised Mother, Most pure Lady, Virgin Theotokos, to thee do I turn the eyes of my soul and body, to thee do I hold out my lame hands and I cry from the depth of my heart: see the faith and humility of my soul; shelter me with thy almighty protection, so that I may be delivered from all afflictions and assaults, and in the hour of my death, visit me, O thou all-blessed, and deliver me from the torment that awaits me because of my sins, that worshipping thee, I may ever cry: "Alleluia."

(This Kontakion is read three times, then Ikos 1 and Kontakion 1 should be read)

Prayers to the most holy Theotokos before her icon "The Protective Veil"

First Prayer

O all-holy Virgin, Mother of the Lord of hosts on high, Queen of heaven and earth and almighty Defender of our city and country! Hear the song of praise and thanksgiving of thine unworthy servants and bring our prayer up to the throne of thy God and Son, that He would be merciful towards our unrighteousness, and would give His grace to those who honour thy name and venerate with faith and love thy wonder-working icon. For we are not worthy of His forgiveness unless thou, O Lady, wouldst move Him by entreaties to be merciful to us, for it is possible for thee to obtain anything by asking Him. Therefore we resort to thee as thou art our prompt and true Protector: hear us who pray to thee, shield us with thine almighty veil and obtain by asking from thy God and Son zeal and vigilant care for the souls for our pastors, wisdom and strength for our mayors, righteousness and impartiality for our judges, understanding and humble wisdom for our mentors, love and harmony for the married, obedience for our children, patience for those who have been offended, fear of God for those that offend, stoutheartedness for the afflicted, temperance for those that rejoice, and for all of us the spirit of understanding and piety, the spirit of mercy and meekness, the spirit of chastity and truth. Yea, O all-holy Lady, be merciful towards thy powerless people: gather together the dispersed, set on the right path those that have gone astray, uphold the aged, make the young chaste, bring up the children and take care of us all by thy merciful protection. Save us from the depth of sin and clear the eyes of our hearts to see the path of salvation. Be merciful to us both here and yonder, during our life's journey on this earth and at the Last Judgement of thy Son; and make our fathers and brothers who have departed this life in faith and repentance to live the eternal life with the angels and all the saints. For thou, O Lady, art the glory of those in heaven and the hope of those on earth. Thou art the first after God, the hope and Defender of all who resort to thee with faith. Therefore we pray to thee, and to thee as to our almighty Helper, do we commend ourselves and one another, now and for ever and unto the ages of ages. Amen.

Second Prayer

O my most blessed Queen, my holy Hope, shelter of the lost and protector of strangers, helper of the poor and protective veil of those in temptations, see my misfortune, see my sorrow: I am surrounded by temptations and there is no one to guard me against them. Therefore help me, thyself, as I am feeble also, guide me as I am a stranger also; instruct me as I also have strayed; heal me and save me as I also am hopeless. I have no other help, no advocate, no comforter, besides thee, o Mother of all the afflicted and heavy laden! Take care of me, a sinner, **whom sickness has prostrated,**@ and shield me with thy holy Veil, that I may be delivered from all the ills surrounding me and may ever praise thy Name that all men sing. Amen.

Troparion to the Protective Veil of the most holy Theotokos, tone 4

Today the faithful celebrate in light, being illumined by thy visit, Mother of God and gazing at thy most pure image, we say with emotion: shield us by thy honourable Veil and deliver us from all evil by pleading with thy Son, Christ, our God, to save our souls.

Exaltation

We magnify thee, most holy Virgin, and we venerate thy honourable Veil, for Saint Andrew saw thee in the air, praying for us to Christ.

Acathistos Hymn in Honour
of the Icon of the Theotokos
"Smolenskaya" or "Hodigitria" (She who shows the way)

Kontakion 1

To thee, chosen from all generations, Queen of Heaven and earth, most holy Theotokos Hodigitria, we, thy servants, being saved from the eternal death by the Grace of Christ our God, Who was born from thee, and by thy motherly entreaties to Him, bring our grateful song. And we plead to thee, our merciful Defender: deliver us from all misfortunes and afflictions and guide us to the Kingdom of Heaven that we may call out to thee: "Rejoice, Theotokos Hodigitria, the Hope of Christians!"

Ikos 1

We cry to thee, o Most Pure, the Archangel's greeting: Rejoice, Grace-giving Hodigitria, Mary, and fill us with spiritual joy, that with reverence in our soul and with a pure heart we may call to thee, who gave birth to Christ, our God and Saviour, the following words:
Rejoice, thou who art shielded by the favour of God the Father;
Rejoice, Virgin Mother of God the Son.
Rejoice, thou who art the holy dwelling of God the Holy Spirit;
Rejoice, thou who art the manifestation of the mystery of the Trinity.
Rejoice, thou who dost make the angelic minds wonder;
Rejoice, thou who art the adornment of human kind.
Rejoice, thou who hast united heaven and earth;
Rejoice, thou who hast opened the gates of paradise to those born on earth.
Rejoice, thou who art the ladder to heaven;
Rejoice, thou who art the vessel that received God.
Rejoice, unconsumed burning Bush;

Rejoice, most holy Bread.
Rejoice, Theotokos Hodigitria, the Hope of Christians!

Kontakion 2

Having seen the icon of thy most holy countenance, o Theotokos Virgin, that the all-praised evangelist Luke painted, thou dost spake with thy most pure mouth: "My Grace and my strength will stay with this icon". As we came to know such a promise of thine, we reverently honour thy most holy image, o Lady, and we sing to thy Son and God: "Alleluia."

Ikos 2

Having seen thy benevolence towards thine icon, the honourable apostle Luke granted it as a blessing and sanctification to the Church of Antioch, where it was later called "She who shows the way" and became famous for its Divine miracles. Thanking thee, most good Lady for this likeness of thy most pure countenance that thou hast given us for our comfort, we zealously cry to thee:
Rejoice, Queen of those in heaven and those on earth;
Rejoice, Lady of angels and of mankind.
Rejoice, thou who art the pacifier of the world;
Rejoice, thou who dost put an end to the ancient enmity.
Rejoice, pillar of virginity;
Rejoice, depth of humility.
Rejoice, thou who art dressed in the sun;
Rejoice, thou who dost shine with Divine glory.
Rejoice, Mother of the Light that never sets;
Rejoice, sweetness of the heavenly paradise.
Rejoice, fragrant garden of Christ;
Rejoice, litter of the Great King.
Rejoice, Theotokos Hodigitria, the Hope of Christians!

Kontakion 3

The most amazing miracles were performed by God's Power through thine icon, Lady Mother of God, when it was brought to Constantinople and placed in the glorious church of Blachernae: it gave sight to the blind and it cured all diseases by the power of thy Grace, Theotokos, and we call to the God Who brought glory to thee: "Alleluia."

Ikos 3

Thou hast been an imperious Defender of Constantinople, Theotokos Virgin, and when powerful and skilful enemies attacked the city, it received in abundance miraculous help from thy holy icon Hodigitria. Therefore we pray to thee, o all-good Theotokos: just as in ancient times thou hast many times saved that city from perishing, save also us, humble ones, from the eternal death by thy maternal pleading with Christ God, so that we may gratefully cry to thee:
Rejoice, robust guard of Constantinople;
Rejoice, Grace-giving treasure of the church of Blachernae.
Rejoice, thou who dost overcome impious armies;
Rejoice, thou who dost put to shame the enemies of Orthodoxy.
Rejoice, always triumphant Leader of the children of Christ;
Rejoice, prompt Helper of those in sorrow who resort to thee.
Rejoice, zealous Defender of those calling prayerfully to thee;
Rejoice, Helper of saints endowed with God's wisdom who spread the Good Message of Christ.
Rejoice, praise of women and the glory of virgins;
Rejoice, pillar of cloud, which dost moderate the sultriness of passions.
Rejoice, fiery pillar, which dost dispel the gloom of sins.

Rejoice, Theotokos Hodigitria, the Hope of Christians!
Kontakion 4

In a storm thou, Lady, hast smashed the ships of the most proud Kagan, who wanted to conquer thy city, and thou hast granted the Christians victory over him through thine icon Hodigitria, which shone with rays of heavenly light for the Orthodox warriors; and everyone could see that thou art the true imperious Leader of Constantinople and would praise thy favours and miracles, singing to God the Saviour: "Alleluia."

Ikos 4

Having heard of thy most glorious miracles, Theotokos Virgin, that thou hast manifested in Constantinople through thine icon, we wonder how this icon, which was carried along the streets of the city, ruled over those who carried it and directed their feet according to thy will; now, Lady, do direct our feet on the path of fulfilling Christ's commandments and teach us to carry out faithfully the holy Will of thy Son and God, so that we may cry to thee:
Rejoice, inextinguishable candle;
Rejoice, star which never sets.
Rejoice, thou who dost shine with Divine light;
Rejoice, thou who dost enlighten by thy Grace the souls of the faithful.
Rejoice, fragrance of Christ's peace;
Rejoice, sanctification of the earth.
Rejoice, cup that pours out joy to the entire world;
Rejoice, source that sheds eternal sweetness.
Rejoice, beautifully adorned palace of the King of Kings;
Rejoice, thou who art more beautiful than paradise;
Rejoice, thou who art brighter than the morning light.

Rejoice, Theotokos Hodigitria, the Hope of Christians!

Kontakion 5

Thine icon, Lady Mother of God, like a Divine star, was brought by thy favour, from Constantinople to Russia, and it was granted to the city of Smolensk as a source of Divine Grace. Therefore we thank thee, all-merciful Lady, and sing to God Who is glorified in the Trinity: "Alleluia."

Ikos 5

Having seen thy most glorious defence of the city of Smolensk, most pure Lady, we praise thy great mercy, that has miraculously saved this city from ravage by Batu: the Divine voice came out of thy icon, sending God's servant Mercurius to challenge the leader of Batu's army to single combat; with his sword Mercurius stabbed the leader and saved thy city from fire. Thou didst later crown him with the martyr's crown; therefore allow us, under the protection of his prayers in heaven, to call upon thee without being condemned:
Rejoice, thou who hast strengthened Christ's martyr Mercurius, to fulfil a heroic deed on the battlefield;
Rejoice, thou who hast inspired him by the voice from thy holy icon.
Rejoice, thou who hast crowned him like another David, after defeating Goliath;
Rejoice, thou who art a strong defence of the city of Smolensk.
Rejoice, thou who hast saved thy city from ruin;
Rejoice, thou who dost Deliver from defeat and imprisonment.
Rejoice, thou who art the Grace-giving consolation of Russia;
Rejoice, thou who art the Divine adornment of the Christian Church.

Rejoice, eternal joy of those who love thee;
Rejoice, consolation of sorrow.
Rejoice, healing of the sick;
Rejoice, encouragement of the despondent.
Rejoice, Theotokos Hodigitria, the Hope of Christians!

Kontakion 6

The Russian land receives thy favours and miracles, most pure Virgin, Theotokos, and the city of Smolensk stands out vividly, having in its possession thy miracle-working icon, which cures all diseases and gives health to all the sick. Therefore we reverently honour thy all-healing image, all-good Lady, and praising it like a pledge of thy benevolence to us, we cry to God: "Alleluia."

Ikos 6

Thou dost shine in the land of Russia, most pure Lady, by the rays of the Divine miracles which come from thy holy icon. In ancient times our fathers turned to it when in illness and afflictions and were always helped. Following them we also turn to thee, and kissing lovingly and reverently thy miracle working image, we pray to thee:
Relieve our sorrows, cure our diseases, that we may call to thee:
Rejoice, staff from ancient times;
Rejoice, defender of the widows.
Rejoice, care of the orphans;
Rejoice, upbringing of the infants.
Rejoice, provider of the poor;
Rejoice, liberation of the prisoners.
Rejoice, comfort of the grieving;
Rejoice, pillar and support of virginity.

Rejoice, protector of the monks;
Rejoice, mentor of the nuns.
Rejoice, strength of those fasting;
Rejoice, teacher of the zealous ascetics.
Rejoice, Theotokos Hodigitria, the Hope of Christians!

Kontakion 7

Wishing to grant to the city of Moscow the Grace of thy holy icon, all-merciful Lady, thou hast favoured its move from Smolensk to Moscow, that being there, it would glorify itself by many miracles. And when, by the entreaties of the citizens of Smolensk, thy holy image was returning to their city, along the way followed by thy icon Hodigitria, a cloister for virgins was established in thy name. Shielded there by thy miracle-working icon, and full of faith and love, we sing an incessant song to God: "Alleluia."

Ikos 7

The newly created convent in Moscow reverently honours the holy copy of thy miracle-working icon Hodigitria, which grants unspeakable favours to the faithful. It shields the orthodox people which thou dost comfort and confirm in fasting and praying, prompting them to praise incessantly thy motherly favours and call to thee gratefully:
Rejoice, Queen loved by God;
Rejoice, Lady, who came to love God.
Rejoice, the only highly favoured amongst women;
Rejoice, joy of those in the heavens.
Rejoice, defender of those on earth;
Rejoice, thou who dost put demons to shame;
Rejoice, thou who dost trample upon hell;

Rejoice, thou who art strengthened by the strength of the God of Hosts.
Rejoice, thou who art invested with power in heaven and on earth;
Rejoice, good Helper of those who fight the passions of the flesh by chastity.
Rejoice, merciful Comforter of those living in fasting and silence.
Rejoice, Theotokos Hodigitria, the Hope of Christians!

Kontakion 8

Thou dost mitigate our earthly journey, full of sorrows and storms, Theotokos, by thy motherly care for us, and in the days of affliction thou dost render thy holy help for our salvation. We remember and acknowledge, o Lady, thy defence, when the Gauls ruined the land of Russia and invested the city of Moscow: thou hast allowed to take thy holy icon Hodigitria from Smolensk to the Russian army to encourage the orthodox warriors, and thou hast granted them a glorious victory, by thy plea before thy Son and God, to Whom we sing: "Alleluia."

Ikos 8

Full of mercy and favour, the all-good Mother of God has gloriously granted help and victory to the Russian-Orthodox warriors. And the Gauls, dishonoured, were driven out of our Fatherland: when we no longer had any hope of salvation, for even our capital was invested and in ruins, thou hast crowned us with a miraculous victory. Always remembering thy defence, we cry our praises to thee:
Rejoice, thou who hast delivered our Russian land from the invasion of foreigners;

Rejoice, thou who hast put to shame and driven back those proud of their power.
Rejoice, All-powerful Victor of the armies of invaders with a strange creed;
Rejoice, imperious Assistant of the orthodox host.
Rejoice, thou who hast abided benevolently in thy icon that was with the Russian warriors;
Rejoice, thou who hast miraculously sanctified their regiments.
Rejoice, thou who hast strengthened the exhausted with power from above;
Rejoice, thou who hast given thy holy help to the helpless.
Rejoice, just Defender of the offended;
Rejoice, reliable Hope of the hopeless.
Rejoice, Comfort of the sorrowful;
Rejoice, Theotokos Hodigitria, the Hope of Christians!

Kontakion 9

All the faithful look, with joy and comfort, at thy holy image, where thou dost point with emotion at the Divine Infant Christ. And we pray to thee, o all-good one, to the Mother of the Ruler, Who upholds all and everything in His hand: look at us, and move the Lord by thine entreaties, that He would have mercy on us, unworthy ones. Teach us, o Lady, to pray to Him in the right way, and to sing to Him without being condemned with unsullied mouth and pure heart the song of the Angels: "Alleluia."

Ikos 9

Our eloquent tongue is not enough to glorify as is due the multitude of thy miracles, Theotokos Hodigitria that thou hast manifested through thine holy icon and dost continue

to manifest constantly to thy faithful ones. Therefore, being a true Good Mother, accept our faith and zeal: thou dost know our love for thee, which sets our heart on fire and hear benevolently these simple praises:
Rejoice, Eternal Virgin, which was gladdened by the Glad Tidings;
Rejoice, Unwedded Bride.
Rejoice, city of God the Word;
Rejoice, dwelling of the Holiest of the Holy.
Rejoice, thou who dost reign eternally with thy Son, the King of Heaven;
Rejoice, thou who dost dispose of motherly boldness towards Him.
Rejoice, thou who dost hear benevolently the prayers of the faithful;
Rejoice, thou who dost give in return thy Divine love to those who love thee.
Rejoice, adornment of the heavenly Zion;
Rejoice, defender of the earthly world.
Rejoice, city of our salvation, to which we resort;
Rejoice, holy mountain, glorified by God's descent.
Rejoice, Theotokos Hodigitria, the Hope of Christians!

Kontakion 10

Save us from eternal death, o Lady, by thy motherly intercession before Christ God, and let us see thee in the hour of our death, keeping away from our soul the claws of the fierce ruler of this world; may we by thy holy Assistance escape his traps and be taken to the Kingdom of Heaven to sing ever joyfully to God, the Lover of mankind: "Alleluia."

Ikos 10

Thou art a protecting wall for the virgins, and a zealous Assistance of all who strive to find virginity and purity. We plead with thee, o Most Pure one: cleanse our hearts from all sinful filth and adorn our souls with chastity and purity that we may stay unharmed from all the temptations of the world, the flesh and the devil, and may deserve to sing to thee the following words:
Rejoice, kind fosterer of virgins;
Rejoice, good Guardian of orphans.
Rejoice, quiet shelter of those seized by passions;
Rejoice, reliable refuge for those troubled by temptations.
Rejoice, thou who dost reward the ascetics, who strive for chastity;
Rejoice, comrade-in-Arms of those who struggle with invisible enemies.
Rejoice, merciful Visitor of those wrongly condemned;
Rejoice, good Comforter of the slandered.
Rejoice, divine Liberator of those imprisoned and in exile;
Rejoice, all-powerful Protector of all that labour and are heavy laden.
Rejoice, thou who dost move by thy entreaties the Righteous Judge;
Rejoice, thou who dost reconcile the sinners with God.
Rejoice, Theotokos Hodigitria, the Hope of Christians!

Kontakion 11

Being unspeakably merciful and hearing the singing, full of emotion, of thy faithful servants, satiate us, most pure Mother-Virgin, with the imperishable nourishment of God's Word and teach us to always fulfil the life-giving commandments of our Lord. Move Him by thy entreaties, our all-good Intercessor, that He may grant us, unworthy ones, His favour and let us inherit His most light and most blissful Kingdom, where all the saints sing to Him the song of praise: "Alleluia."

Ikos 11

Thou dost illumine us by the light rays of thy Grace-giving miracles, Theotokos Hodigitria and thou dost send spiritual comfort to God's servants through thy holy icon Hodigitria. And may the flow of its healing gifts for us, sinners, not grow scarce, that we may gratefully cry to thee and praise thee:
Rejoice, thou who hast given birth to the imperishable Lamb and Shepherd;
Rejoice, thou who dost combine in thyself virginity and the glory of Motherhood.
Rejoice, lily of virginity that leads to the pure and virgin life;
Rejoice, thou who hast manifested thy holy love for God's elect;
Rejoice, thou who dost reveal the heavenly Commandments;
Rejoice, thou who hast honoured Saint Sergius of Radonezh by thy visit.
Rejoice, thou who, by a command from thine icon, hast sent Saint Cyril to the White Lake;
Rejoice, thou who hast strengthened Saint Sabbatios of Solovki in his ascetic solitude.
Rejoice, thou who, by thine icon, hast done a great favour to the holy Prelate Mithrophan of Voronezh.
Rejoice, Protective Veil and Provider of the Christian monasteries and convents;
Rejoice, secret Mentor of Christ's servants in the world.
Rejoice, Theotokos Hodigitria, the Hope of Christians!

Kontakion 12

It is God's Grace that works the miracles which are gloriously manifested by thy holy image, o most blessed Theotokos Virgin. Illumine also our souls by It, dispel the sinful gloom by the brightness of the Sun of Truth: Christ, and let us live this temporary life in the light of His God pleasing commands, in piety and purity and let us be favoured by the eternal bliss, singing for God together with the elect: "Alleluia."

Ikos 12

Singing thy miracles, Theotokos, we propagate thy favours, we glorify thy innumerable generous gifts and kneeling before thy miracle working icon, we pray to thee faithfully and lovingly: be our good Guide on the path to the city of light, Jerusalem in the heavens, that we may see thee, looking benevolently at us from the height of thy Divine Glory, and sing to thee together with the saints :
Rejoice, our most holy Joy;
Rejoice, our good Queen.
Rejoice, thou who hast adopted us at the Cross of thy Son and God;
Rejoice, thou who hast shown us thy Motherly love.
Rejoice, thou who dost fulfil our good wishes in a wondrous way;
Rejoice, thou who dost promptly answer humble prayers.
Rejoice, thou who dost protect us safely by thy glorious garment.
Rejoice, our almighty Assistant in the hour of our death;
Rejoice, our imperious Defender during the ordeals after death.

Rejoice, gratuitous healing of our bodies;
Rejoice, salvation of our souls.
Rejoice, Theotokos Hodigitria, the Hope of Christians!

Kontakion 13

O all-praised Mother, Queen, all-merciful Virgin Theotokos Hodigitria! Accept our small entreaty and bring it to thy Son, appealing as a mother to His Goodness, that He would have mercy on us, sinners and unworthy ones, and for the sake of thy all-powerful intercession would deliver us from eternal torment, accept us in the Kingdom of Heaven and let us sing there to God together with the Angels: "Alleluia."
(This Kontakion is read three times, and then Ikos 1 and Kontakion 1 should be read.)

Prayers to the most holy Theotokos before her icon "Hodigitria" or "Smolenskaya"

First Prayer

O most Wondrous and above all creatures elevated Queen, Theotokos, Mother of our Heavenly King, Christ God, most pure Hodigitria Mary! Hear us, the sinners and unworthy ones, praying to thee at this moment and kneeling before thy most pure Image, say with emotion: lead us away from the ditch of passions, o most good Lady, deliver us from any grief and sorrow, guard us against any misfortune and malicious slander, and against unjust and fierce calumny of the fiend. For thou, o Grace-giving Mother, can protect thy people from any ill and provide them with any favour and save them: besides thee we, sinners, have no warm Intercessor in our misfortunes and afflictions. Move by thy entreaties, most holy Lady, thy Son and our God, that He would grant us the Kingdom of Heaven: therefore we always glorify thee, as the Cause of our salvation and extol the holy and magnificent Name of the Father, the Son and the Holy Spirit, one God, glorified and worshipped in the Trinity, in the ages of ages.

Second Prayer

To whom should I cry, o Lady? To whom, besides thee, Lady Theotokos, Queen of Heaven should I resort? Who else would listen to my moaning and sighs, besides thee, most chaste, the Hope of Christians and the refuge of sinners? Listen favourably to my entreaty, Mother of my God; do not reject me, who asks for thy help; hear my groaning and inspire the cry of my heart, o Lady Theotokos, the Queen. And grant me joy in my soul, strengthen me, impatient, despondent and negligent, in praising thee. Make me understand and teach me how I should pray to thee and do not abandon me because of my grumbling and impatience, but be my protecting veil and defence in my life and lead me to the quiet shelter of that blissful rest and reckon me among thy chosen flock and favour me there to sing and to praise thee unto the ages. Amen.

Troparion, tone 4

Now we all, sinful and humble ones, diligently resort to the Theotokos, and kneeling before her crying in repentance from the depth of our soul: Lady, help us; have mercy on us, endeavour to save us, as we perish in the multitude of our sins; do not send back thy servants with empty hands, for thou art our only hope.

Glory to the Father and to the Son and to the Holy Spirit, both now and ever, and unto the ages of ages. Amen.

We, unworthy ones, will never fail, Theotokos, to praise thy miracles. If thou dost not intercede for us, praying, who else could deliver us from so many misfortunes? Who could keep us free even up till now? We won't betray thee, o Lady, for thou dost save thy servants from all fierce afflictions.
Kontakion, tone 4

O protection of Christians who cannot be put to shame, most constant mediator to the Creator, o despise not the pleading voices of those who have sinned; but be thou quick, o good one, to come to our aid, who in faith cry unto thee: Hasten to

intercede, and speed thou to plead, thou who dost ever protect, O Theotokos, them that honour thee.
Kontakion, tone 6

We have no other help, we have no other hope but thee, o Lady: help us, for we lay our hope onto thee and we boast of thee: we are thy servants, do not put us to shame.

Acathistos Hymn in Honour
of the Icon of the Theotokos
"Unfading Blossom"

Kontakion 1

O most blessed Theotokos Virgin, the joy and the refuge of all the Christians: honouring thy most pure image, we sing to thee a song of praise, we bring thee our needs, grief and tears. Thou art our meek Defender, all our earthly sorrows and afflictions are known to thee, so accept our prayerful sighs, help us and deliver us from all misfortunes, for we call unto thee incessantly and with emotion:
Rejoice, Mother of God, Unfading Blossom.

Ikos 1

Like God's blessing and like a gift from heaven, long awaited, obtained by incessant prayer, thou hast been sent, Theotokos, to thy righteous and intensely glad parents Joachim and Anne. While, o God's chosen child, thou hast left the parental bosom, and like an inextinguishable lamp of faith, like a fragrant censer, hast appeared humbly before the threshold of the Lord, and the power of the One on High lifted thee up to the very entrance, brought thee into the Holy of Holies and opened for thee the innermost mysteries of Heaven.
O most merciful Theotokos Virgin! Open also our hearts to praise thee and lift up our prayer to Thy Son and our God that we may call unto thee:
Rejoice, unattainable purity and unspeakable meekness;
Rejoice, thou who art extolled for thy humility.
Rejoice, inexhaustible source of love;
Rejoice, vessel chosen by God.
Rejoice, our zealous Defender.
Rejoice, Mother of God, Unfading Blossom.

Kontakion 2

O most holy Virgin Mary, we are bowed down by our sinful designs and shameful deeds, our heart is seized by the coldness of life, our eyes are laden with a sinful sleep. But thou, o Unfading Blossom, cleanse us with the morning dew, warm us with the sun of love and mercy. Raise us up to the Lord, o Lady, from the earthly dust, that we may bring Him our humble entreaty and cry to Him: "Alleluia."

Ikos 2

The angel Gabriel was sent from God unto a city of Galilee, named Nazareth and he has brought thee, o most pure Virgin, the holy annunciation, saying: "Hail, thou that art highly favoured, the Lord is with thee: blessed art thou among women: thou hast found favour with God." (Luke 1:26,30)
While we, being unworthy, seeing such greatness, cry to thee from our humble hearts:
Rejoice, thou who art blessed among women;
Rejoice, thou who hast found favour with God and art extolled higher than the angels.
Rejoice, for thou hast conceived a Son, Who will inherit the throne of David, His forefather in the flesh;
Rejoice, thou who hast kindled the inextinguishable light for the hearts in darkness.
Rejoice, thou who dost open for us the doors of eternal happiness.
Rejoice, Mother of God, Unfading Blossom.

Kontakion 3

Perturbed by our sorrows, we spend the days of our life vainly and in sadness. But thee, o Blessed one, enlighten our souls by thy annunciation, fill our hearts with humility, that we may bow our heads and say: "Behold the servants of the Lord; be it unto us according to thy will!" For we sing hourly to thee, Unfading Blossom, and to the One, Who is born from thee: "Alleluia."

Ikos 3

"And Mary arose in those days, and went into the hill country with haste, into a city of Juda; and entered into the house of Zacharias, and saluted Elisabeth. And it came to pass, that, when Elisabeth heard the salutation of Mary, the babe leaped in her womb; and Elisabeth was filled with the Holy Ghost. And she spake out with a loud voice, and said: and whence is this to me, that the mother of my Lord should come to me?" (Luke 1:39-43)
O most pure Virgin! Visit also us, powerless and wretched ones, and raise our sighs like the fragrant smoke of a censer to the throne of the Most High, that we may sing to thee in the fullness of our grateful heart:
Rejoice, for the Lord hath looked upon the low estate of his handmaiden;
Rejoice, for all generations shall call thee blessed.
Rejoice, for the Mighty hath done to thee great things;
Rejoice, source of life and immortality.
Rejoice, Mother of God, Unfading Blossom.

Kontakion 4

O Unfading Blossom! O fragrant Beauty! Appear in our sorrowful life, move thy Son by thy entreaties that He may guard us against every affliction and sorrow, anger and sigh, and give peace to our hearts; that He may grant us what we ask from Him, to everyone according to their needs and may shield us by His inexhaustible favour. While we, hoping for thy all-mighty defence, honour in our soul our Lord and cry to Him: "Alleluia."

Ikos 4

An Angel of the Lord has announced great joy to the shepherds, who watched their flocks by night: the Lord Christ is born in Bethlehem, David's city, He is wrapped in swaddling clothes and laid in a manger. O most pure Mother, who hast given birth to thy first born Child, hear our song:
Rejoice, Virgin Theotokos, for the Light of reason which never sets began to shine for the world through thee;
Rejoice, star that shows us the way in the dark.
Rejoice, dawn of the mysterious day;
Rejoice, rebirth of our souls.
Rejoice, safe refuge and prompt Assistance in sorrows;
Rejoice, lily of Paradise.
Rejoice, all-praised Virgin;
Rejoice, meek dove that gave birth to the only Merciful.
Rejoice, Mother of God, Unfading Blossom.

Kontakion 5

Behold, the King of the World comes: behold, the secret Sacrifice is accomplished; the angels sing in the heavens: "Glory to God on high!"
The Saviour of the world is born now. Christ comes: a great Divine mystery. God has put on flesh and we, His unworthy servants, having put aside all earthly concerns, praise God together with the angels in fear and joy; we honour thee, o Mother of God, like the shepherds and the magi, and we call incessantly to thy Divine Son: "Alleluia."

Ikos 5

Behold, the righteous Simeon came guided by the Spirit into the temple and he took up the Infant Jesus in his arms, and blessed God, and said: "Lord, now lettest Thou Thy servant depart in peace, according to Thy word!" (Lk 2:27-29) And thee, Mother, Mary, the sword shall pierce through thy own soul, that the thoughts of many hearts may be revealed. (Lk. 2: 35) While we, being saved by thee, cry:
Rejoice, blessed One, who transforms great sorrow into joy;
Rejoice, eternal well of motherly love and tenderness.
Rejoice, Mother of our God, who hast known the greatest joy and the greatest suffering because of Thy son.
Rejoice, Queen of the world.
Rejoice, Hope and Consolation for those who weep.
Rejoice, Mother of God, Unfading Blossom.

Kontakion 6

O good Mother, Mary! The ups and downs of life grow intense like a storm of anger; deep abysses open up and are ready to swallow us up; our heart trembles and our joy is darkened. Therefore we plead with thee, meek and merciful one, move thy Son by thy entreaties that He would help us, who are lost and grieving in our sorrows; stave off from us all the misfortunes and dangers; teach us how to observe His eternal truth. And at the end of our life show us a quiet, still refuge and vouchsafe us to cry together with Simeon the God-receiver: "Lord, now lettest Thou Thy servant depart in peace!" Do help us, o Unfading Blossom! Don't leave us alone and save all those that call unto God: "Alleluia."

Ikos 6

And the Child grew and increased in spirit and grace. And his mother kept all these sayings lovingly in her heart. Sorrowful and sad thou sought him among thy kinsfolk and acquaintance, when thou didst return from the feast in Jerusalem. With great joy thou didst find Him in the temple, sitting in the midst of the doctors, who were astonished at His Divine reason. (Luke 2:43-48) O our most pure Meekness! O sweetest heart, which warms the whole world with love! Hear us, who cry unto thee:

Rejoice, thou who hast brought up thy Divine Son by thy love;
Rejoice, sweetest heart, who dost warm our cold souls by thy love.
Rejoice, wise mentor of parents' hearts;
Rejoice, infallible protective wall for our children.
Rejoice, protecting Veil and Refuge for the powerless and the lost;
Rejoice, Guard of chastity and virginity.

Rejoice, thou who dost show the honest and righteous way to the meek;
Rejoice, mollifyer of the wicked hearts.
Rejoice, emotion of the good ones.
Rejoice, Mother of God, Unfading Blossom.

Kontakion 7

"Son, why hast thou thus dealt with us?" (Luke 2: 48) thus His mother asked her Son Jesus, feeling amazed at seeing Him sitting in the temple between the most proud and vain high priests of the Jews, and revealing to them the Divine Wisdom, opening for them the Divine Revelation. O good Mother, be favourably disposed to our offspring, pray for them to thy Son and our God that He would reveal to them the light of true Theology; shield them with the edge of thy fragrant protective veil; enlighten our sons and daughters by the light of reason; strengthen their bodies and souls; keep them in the fear of God, obedient to their parents and pure of soul; favour them to grow up for God's glory and the happiness of the land of our forefathers. O inextinguishable lamp of love, anoint them with the balm of thy favour; warm them with the meekness of thy eyes; shield them by the raiment of thy Maternity. O Unfading Blossom! Lying prostrate at thy feet, with firm faith, unshakeable hope and intense distress in our heart, we cry to God incessantly: "Alleluia."

Ikos 7

O warm intercessor for this adulterous and sinful generation! At thy request, at the wedding in Cana of Galilee, thy Son and our God performed His first miracle and changed water into wine. Move by thine entreaties thy Son also now, o Mother of God, that He may perform a miracle also on us, let Him trans-

form our days, full of lies, resentment and tears into the joy of revival, into the happiness of love and truth; let Him strengthen in us the source of Divine Light: Holy God, Three in One. Let Him expel from our hearts all that is evil and impure. O unattainable Purity and unspeakable Mercy! Bend thy ear to our prayer and favour us to call to thee:
Rejoice, bright Light of love and forgiveness;
Rejoice, divine Vessel of eternal bliss.
Rejoice, zealously praying Intercessor for us before God;
Rejoice, thou who dost bring promptly our requests to God's throne.
Rejoice, for listening to thee, thy Son works miracles, giving joy to humankind.
Rejoice, Mother of God, Unfading Blossom.

Kontakion 8

There is no love, truth has vanished, lie and hostility, anger and hatred have been sowed into man" heart. Brother rises up against brother, children against their parents, and parents against their children. O Merciful God! Who defiled thy wondrous harvest, who sowed tares and thistles among the wheat? (Matthew 13:25) Thy wrath is righteous, now also the axe is laid at the root of the trees: (Matt. 3:10) but lo and behold: thy Mother, the zealous Intercessor for the world, kneels before Thee. O, the greatest Love and the most fragrant heart! Turn away from us God's wrath, justly coming down on us because of our sins; strengthen those who love us that neither persecution nor hard times would shake them; make those who hate us and inflict misfortunes on us understand; forgive our enemies who do not know what they are doing, mollify their wicked hearts and illumine their darkness by the light of Christ's love, and turn their malice and hatred into a feeling of shame and repentance. O fragrant Blossom!

Our vessels are empty; we do not have the oil of the deeds of virtue and the lamps of our faith are almost extinguished by the storms of life. Have therefore mercy on us: fill our hearts with the gladness of pure joy; renew us spiritually that we may sing to God in gratefulness: "Alleluia."

Ikos 8

Divine Teacher, Thou hast been fully with those on earth and at the same time in no way have left the Highest: Thou hast healed the sick, resurrected the dead, cleansed the leprous, and filled the entire world with Thy love, Thou the Meek Sufferer! Lo and behold, Thou dost hang, nailed to the cross, between two villains, and all the people have been scolding and mocking you, together with the soldiers and the princes. While thou, the sorrowful Mother, hast bowed thy head, standing near the cross of thy Son and the sword has pierced thy heart. We honour the grief of thy motherly heart and we cry unto thee from the depth of our soul:
Rejoice, sweetest Virgin Mary, for thy sorrow will turn into joy, which no one will be able to take from thee;
Rejoice, thou who hast undergone the greatest torment, when seeing thy Son, bleeding to death on the cross, humiliated, crucified and spurned.
Rejoice, as thou art called the Queen of the world and dost sit on the right side of the throne of thy Son and God, and our Lord Jesus Christ;
Rejoice, for through the sorrow of thy heart thou hast washed by thy tears the sorrow of the entire world and the sins of all men.
Rejoice, meek One, for thy Son will resurrect, having trampled down the sting of death and the Light of His Resurrection will shine in the ages of ages;
Rejoice, Theotokos, heavenly image of purity and good.

Rejoice, Mother of God, Unfading Blossom.

Kontakion 9

God conceived such a love for the world that He gave His First Born Son that everyone who believes in Him will not perish but will find eternal life. And lo and behold: ungrateful and wicked people have nailed Him, like a villain, to the Cross. And we, seeing this, and being seized with terror, cry: "Lord, be merciful to us, the sinners!" (Lk. 18:13) For it is because of our transgressions that now Thou dost endure terrible torments. O sorrowful Mother, do not turn away thy countenance from us, break our sinful ties, cleanse our hearts from the crafty passions and lusts that we with spiritual zeal, may burn like a candle of repentance, before the cross of thy Divine Son, pleading incessantly together with the penitent thief: "Remember me when Thou comest into thy kingdom!" (Luke 23:42)
Set our feet on the path of fulfilling the Lord's commandments, Theotokos; wash our sins away, make us better, raise us to the bright Light which never sets, that we may call to God: "Alleluia."

Ikos 9

"It has come to pass! Father, into Thy hands I commend my spirit." (Luke 23:48,49) O most pure Mother! Do thou hear how the earth did quake from sorrow, and the rocks rent, the graves were opened, the dead arose and the veil of the temple was rent in twain from the top to the bottom. (Matt. 27: 51-53) Thou dost see how darkness covered the whole land and people in fear and trembling smote their breasts saying: "Truly this was the Son of God!" While we, astonished by this

miracle and professing thy Son as the true Son of God, faithfully cry to thee:
Rejoice, Mother of God, for all the words that thou hast kept in thy heart have come true;
Rejoice, Grace giving Virgin, Dawn that never sets;
Rejoice, Day which never ends, golden Light.
Rejoice, Sanctuary of the great mystery.
Rejoice, Source of our immortality;
Rejoice, Giver of the Divine goodness.
Rejoice, Mother of God, Unfading Blossom.

Kontakion 10

Let all mortal flesh be silent and stand with fear and trembling, and meditate nothing earthly within itself. For the great sacrifice is made to atone for the sins of the world and lo and behold the Saviour of the world is wrapped in fine linen and laid in a new sepulchre by the noble Joseph, while His soul descends to the nethermost regions to shatter the gates of hell and free the dead shackled since ages. And He prophecies to His mother from His sepulchre: "Lament not for Me, Mother, when thou beholdest in the tomb the Son whom thou didst conceive in thy womb, for I shall rise again and glorify Myself; and in that I am God, I will raise in glory the believers who with faith and love do magnify thee. Let us lay aside all that is earthly and vain and prostrate ourselves with pure hearts, before the throne of the King of Glory, crying incessantly: Holy, holy, holy is the Lord Sabaoth!" O Mother of our salvation! Turn also us into participators in the bright Resurrection of thy Son and the eternal bliss, that we may call to God: "Alleluia."

Ikos 10

"Now upon the first day of the week, very early in the morning, the women came unto the sepulchre, bringing the spices which they had prepared, and they found the stone rolled away from the sepulchre. And they entered it, and found not the body of the Lord Jesus.
And the Angel, shining brightly, said unto them: "O women! Do not be afraid, why seek ye the living among the dead: Christ is risen, as He said!" (Luke 24:1- 6) And He has taught all to sing to thee:
Rejoice, Blessed Theotokos Virgin, and again I say: Rejoice, for thy Son is risen from his three days' sojourn in the grave.
Rejoice, for the whole earth rejoices, and all the angels in heaven sing: "Christ is risen from the dead, trampling down death by death, and upon those in the tomb bestowing life!";
Rejoice, Giver of the eternal, endless life.
Rejoice, for through thy love and thy prayers we are delivered from the eternal darkness;
Rejoice, for through thee the bright feast of feasts shines upon us.
Rejoice, for through thee the bright day hath shone forth upon us, let us embrace one another, rejoice at the resurrection in the simplicity of our soul and we will be gladdened with the eternal joy.
Rejoice, Mother of God, Unfading Blossom.

Kontakion 11

O Jerusalem, Jerusalem, thou that killest the prophets! Your heavy crime has been forgiven by the Lord and the Sun of truth which never sets has started to shine in the world. Cleanse also our souls, Meek Virgin! Cleanse our senses that we may see Christ, coming out of the sepulchre; clothe us in the wedding garments that we may joyfully enter Christ's adorned palace, singing to Him who is risen: "Alleluia."

Ikos 11

When the hour of thy departure to God came, o Mother of God, Virgin, Gabriel, the angel of the Lord, shining brightly, appeared before thee and delivered thee the white and unfading lily of paradise. And lo and behold: thou hast accepted humbly and joyfully the Will of the Lord and peacefully passed away, to meet thy Divine Son. O our Intercessor, who tirelessly dost pray for us! O Unfading Blossom of the bright heavenly paradise! Grant also to us, thou the Merciful one, a quiet and painless departure from this earthly world, full of weeping, sighs and sorrow, that we may cry to thee:
Rejoice, Queen of Heaven, elevated by thy Son;
Rejoice, our prompt and trustworthy Intercessor before Him.
Rejoice, all-hymned Virgin, for thy unfading beautiful name is praised from generation to generation;
Rejoice, our quiet and reliable refuge amidst the storms of life.
Rejoice, joyful Mother of God, who dost not forsake us even after thy departure.
Rejoice, Mother of God, Unfading Blossom.

Kontakion 12

O our last, terrible hour! Our heart and all our limbs tremble when we just think of it! How will we forsake our nearest and dearest ones? How will we walk, unrepentant, through the darkness and the shadow of death towards the new life? How will we appear at the Last Judgement of our Creator and God? O our Comforter! O our good Helper! Help us, when all this has come to pass, put thy loving motherly hand on our forehead that our suffering may subside and our soul revive; quieten our anguish at parting from this world, and let the light of the eternal truth shine before our eyes. O most pure Mother! We lay our hope in thee, we pray to thee and we cry to thee: "Alleluia."

Ikos 12

O my soul, my soul! Rise up, why art thou sleeping? The end draws near! Why dost thou still sin? Dost thou not care, prepare thyself? The Lord draws near thy door, what canst thou hope for? What answer canst thou give the Lord, when He will come as a dreadful Judge to judge the earth: thou dost know hour, nor day; the Archangel's trumpet will sound all over the earth, and the dead will rise and all the nations come together. And see, the Son of Man comes on the clouds in full strength and glory. Where are our deeds of virtue? Where is mercy? Where is love? An infinite multitude of our transgressions covers the sky completely. O all-merciful Theotokos! Appear to us on this terrible day and be our Intercessor before thy Son. We lay our hope in thee alone, do not forsake us, sinners. Be our defence and strength for we prostrate ourselves before thy most pure image with warm faith and unshakeable hope, and cry to thee with tears:
Rejoice, lightning that illuminates our darkness;
Rejoice, our defender in the dreadful court of Christ.
Rejoice, thou who dost shield the entire world against sorrows and afflictions with thy protecting veil;
Rejoice, for thou art the Mother of the entire world.
Rejoice, for to thee alone an unspeakable blessing is given to pray for all of us;
Rejoice, thou who dost prepare the eternal joy for thy faithful sons and daughters.

Rejoice, thou who dost perfume us in the ages of ages with thy Unfading Blossom.
Rejoice, Mother of God, Unfading Blossom.

Kontakion 13

O, Unfading Blossom! O, all-praised Mother, Mary, who hast given birth to the Word, which is more holy than all the saints! Accept this our offering, deliver us from all afflictions. Warm us with thy Motherly love, gladden us with the eternal joy. Save us from the eternal torment by thy incessant prayer to thy Son and vouchsafe us the Kingdom of Heaven, who cry to thee ""Alleluia, Alleluia, Alleluia."
(This Kontakion is read three times, then Ikos 1 and Kontakion 1 should be read)

Acathistos Hymn

Prayer to the most holy Theotokos before her icon "Unfading Blossom"

O most holy and chaste Mother Virgin, hope of the Christians and refuge of the sinners! Protect all those who come to thee in their afflictions, hear our cry, bend thy ear to our entreaties. Lady and Mother of our God, do not neglect those asking for thy help and do not reject us, sinners; make us understand and teach us: do not forsake us, thy servants, because of our complaints. Be our Mother and Protector, we entrust ourselves to thy merciful protecting veil. Lead us, sinners, to a quiet and placid life so that we can repent our sins. O Mother, Mary, our good and prompt Defender, shield us by thy intercession. Guard us against our visible and invisible enemies; mollify the hearts of wicked people, rising against us. O Mother of our God and Creator! Thou art the root of virginity and the unfading blossom of purity and chastity, send thy help to us who are powerless, who lose heart and are gripped by the passions of the flesh. Cleanse the eyes of our soul that we may see the ways of God's truth. Strengthen our weak will by the Grace of thy Son that we may fulfil His commandments and be delivered from all misfortunes and afflictions and be acquitted through thy wondrous defence at the dreadful judgement of thy Son, to whom we give glory, honour and adoration now, and always and in the ages of ages.

Troparion, tone 5

Rejoice, God's Bride, secret wand, Unfading flowering Blossom; rejoice, Lady, whose joy fills us and makes us heirs of the eternal life.

ACATHISTOS HYMN IN HONOUR
OF THE ICON OF THE THEOTOKOS
"THE UNCONSUMED BURNING BUSH"

Kontakion 1

To the Victorious Leader, most Pure and by God gladdened Theotokos, who has rejoiced Christ's Church by the appearance of her fiery icon, which protects the faithful against fire, we sing a song of praise. While thou, o Mother of God, whom we call "The Unconsumed burning Bush", having invincible power and great mercy, dost hasten to help us, who ask for thine intercession and deliver us from all afflictions for we call to thee: Rejoice, Grace-giving Unconsumed burning Bush, who guards us against fire.

Ikos 1

The Queen of Angels and of all creation, Our Lady Theotokos, who dost hear the praises of the Angelic choirs, favour also us, made of earth and ashes, to offer Thee words of praise and gratefulness for thy exceeding mercy to humankind. And though we are not worthy of praising thee as it should, do not abhor our poor song of praise, for thou art good: as thy Son hast kindly accepted the two mites of the widow, so thou also dost kindly hear us, who cry to thee affectionately:
Rejoice, thou who hast carried without being burnt the fire of God in thy womb;
Rejoice, thou who hast given birth to the Saviour of fallen humanity.
Rejoice, thou who hast abolished the power of hell by giving birth in all purity;
Rejoice, thou who hast freed Adam and Eve from the ancient curse.
Rejoice, thou who hast served chastely for the incarnation of One in the Trinity;
Rejoice, thou who hast provided the seedless incarnation of the Creator of Heaven and Earth.

Rejoice, Grace-giving Unconsumed Burning Bush, who guards us against fire.

Kontakion 2

Having seen the bush on the Sinai, which was burning without being consumed, Moses was astounded, and then God's Voice came from the bush: loose thy sandals from off thy feet for the ground where thou dost stand is sacred.
Also we, humbly listening, confess the mystery of God the Word's incarnation through the Most Pure Virgin, of which the wonder of the unconsumed burning bush was an omen, and in fear we honour the place of God's manifestation, calling unto the Creator of all: "Alleluia."

Ikos 2

The human mind cannot comprehend the mystery of God's omniscience, Who has determined the redemption of fallen humanity in the Pre-eternal Council of the Threefold Deity; however God's holy prophets, inspired by the Holy Spirit, have foreseen already in ancient times the wonder of wonders, that the Creator will take on the shape of the servant, wanting to save the work of His Hands from eternal death; they have been proclaiming through images and prophesies the coming redemption of humankind by the promised Redeemer. And having given Him His flesh, thou, most Pure, hast been favoured to become the Mother of thy Lord, Who prompts us to cry to thee:
Rejoice, fiery Palace of the One Who sits on the Cherubim;
Rejoice, light-bearing couch of the Ruler of the Seraphim.
Rejoice, bed of the Great King on the top of the mountain of heaven;

Rejoice, animated Throne of the Master of all in heaven and on earth.
Rejoice, consecrated arch of God, greater than the Holy of the Holiest;
Rejoice, golden vessel, in which the saving manna has been prepared: the flesh and blood of the Divine Lamb.
Rejoice, Grace-giving Unconsumed Burning Bush, who guards us against fire.

Kontakion 3

Acting on behalf of the Most High, our good Lady, thou dost tame the power of the element of fire by thy holy icon, and through it thou dost work many miracles in the universe. Therefore Christians honour thee with songs of praise and in unexpected afflictions, most of all when in danger of fire, call to thee through prayers and receive thy help in due time. Therefore we cry gratefully to the King of Glory, Christ, Who glorified thee: "Alleluia."

Ikos 3

Having great love for the people redeemed by the glorious blood of thy Son and God, o most pure Mother of God, thou hast received from Him the power to rule and to defend the Christians: thou art the Guarantor of the sinners in their repentance before the Creator, the Hope for salvation of the hopeless, the prompt Assistant of those in affliction, the One who imperiously calls to account the fallen ones and the Protecting Veil of every Christian community. Rewarding thee with love, our merciful and good-loving Defender, we say to thee these words of humble wisdom:
Rejoice, universal Joy, who dost wipe the tears of suffering and sorrowful eyes;

Rejoice, quiet and good refuge where those seized by the storms of life find their salvation.
Rejoice, all-mighty Theotokos who dost soothe God's wrath, which righteously comes upon us;
Rejoice, thou who dost extinguish the fiery flames with the dew of thy prayers before God the All-Upholder's Throne;
Rejoice, thou who dost protect us from thunder and lightning by thy heavenly intercession;
Rejoice, thou who dost render thy help in due time to every soul that faithfully prays to thee.
Rejoice, Grace-giving Unconsumed Burning Bush, who guards us against fire.

Kontakion 4

When the fiery storm will suddenly fall upon us and its flames will seize our cities and villages, then, all-merciful Lady, hurry to help us who are powerless, protect us by thy glorious icon and deliver us from the fiery punishment, which we justly deserve because of our sins. For thou art our Defender, who never puts us, sinners, to shame; therefore we place our hope in thee and glorifying the power of thy prayers we call to thee Miracle of the world: "Alleluia."

Ikos 4

We see and hear about the great miracles worked by thy icon, our good Queen, which thou hast given us as comfort and protection in our afflictions; lo and behold even the all-consuming fire loses its power when confronted with the Grace-giving power of thy most pure Image. Many, many times we have seen and experienced this and we call thee "The Unconsumed burning Bush" and we sing songs of praise before thine image:

Rejoice, thou who dost pray incessantly to Christ God, inclining Him to be merciful to us;
Rejoice, thou who dost turn away God's wrath, which comes upon us because of our transgressions.
Rejoice, thou who dost protect us from all afflictions by thy glorious raiment;
Rejoice, thou who dost protect by the generous gift of thy Motherly veil our dwellings from thunder and lightning.
Rejoice, all-merciful Hearer of our entreaties in sorrow and afflictions;
Rejoice, our bold and prompt Helper in the days of severe ordeals.
Rejoice, Grace-giving Unconsumed burning Bush, who guards us against fire.

Kontakion 5

Thy most glorious icon, Theotokos Virgin, like the Divine star of the Nativity, shines over the whole world by the multitude of its miracles and illumines the hearts and the souls of men so that they learn about thy great mercy, and thy Motherly good-hearted shield and protection of Christians. Being rejoiced by this we thank Christ God, Who has granted thee, His Mother in the flesh, as Mother in the spirit to us, and we call to Him, with deep emotion: "Alleluia."

Ikos 5

We see thine icon, Lady, as a true Unconsumed burning Bush, which isn't consumed by flames and which protects by its presence our dwellings from fire. Thou hast been given grace from above for thou hast carried in thy womb the power of the fiery nature, without being burnt; and thy most pure image was touched with this Grace, therefore the faithful have named it: "The Unconsumed burning Bush", which image we honour magnificently and cry to thee the song of praise:

Rejoice, inextinguishable candle, which burns eternally as a prayer for us before the Throne of the Lord;

Rejoice, thou who dost kindle also our cold hearts by the fire of God's Love.

Rejoice, thou who dost cool the heat of our passions;

Rejoice, thou who dost send us in moments of sorrow and confusion the thoughts, which are good and useful for our soul.

Rejoice, thou who dost hurry to succour us when we are in poverty and have no one to help us;

Rejoice, thou who dost save us by thy imperious hand from perishing in times of sudden misfortune.

Rejoice, Grace-giving Unconsumed burning Bush, who guards us against fire.

Kontakion 6

The Church tells us of thy miracles, Mother of God, which are more numerous than the sands of the seas and the stars in the heavens: thy name is praised in East and West for thy miracles and there is no city or country where through thee God's power was not manifested for the deliverance and salvation, illumination and healing of the Christians; and most of all thou dost continuously work miracles through thy holy icons, streams of mercy and generous gifts flowing from them to the sick and poor humanity.

Therefore we glorify thee with spiritual songs of praise and we cry to thy Son and our God: "Alleluia."

Ikos 6

Thou dost shine with Divine glory, Virgin and Bride of God, holding in thine arms the Infant and Pre-eternal Lord Jesus Christ and surrounded by the assembly of the angelic hosts, as we see thy image painted on the icon of Moses' Unconsumed burning Bush. Through this icon thou dost grant Graceful gifts to the faithful, thou dost save them from thunder and lightning, thou dost heal the sick and comfort the sorrowful and thou dost give to everyone all that is good and useful for their soul. Therefore we sing to thee incessantly:
Rejoice, for the Assembly of Angels and humankind joyfully celebrate thy Victory;
Rejoice, thou whose glory is above all the praises of heaven and earth.
Rejoice, thou who from heavenly heights dost watch with loving motherly care over the entire universe;
Rejoice, thou who dost give thy blessing to the sorrowful earthly world.
Rejoice, thou who dost not deprive of thy innumerable favours the despised and the outcast;
Rejoice, thou who through the compassion of thy heart dost save the lost from the abyss.
Rejoice, Grace-giving Unconsumed burning Bush, who guards us against fire.

Kontakion 7

The Lord wanting to manifest His love for the humanity redeemed by His Blood, has given us as protector and defender His most Chaste Mother and made her a good and quiet refuge for every embittered and sorrowful Christian soul, which needs help and mercy. Thus knowing about thy merciful help to mankind, our Good Lady, we raise our eyes to thee in our sorrows and hold out our hands in prayer to thee, asking for consolation from thee alone, that thou dost save us by thy intercession from temporary and eternal sorrows, and vouchsafe us to reach the land of the living and share the joy of the saints who sing to God: "Alleluia."

Ikos 7

Thou hast wondrously glorified thy holy icon, called "The Unconsumed burning Bush", o Theotokos Virgin, by which thou dost guard cities and villages from fire and from thunder and lightning and thou dost bless the houses of the faithful, where the likeness of thy most pure countenance is honoured. Therefore we gladly receive thy Grace-giving image as a precious gift, and honour it as one ought and gratify thee by the following songs of praise:
Rejoice, vessel of healing, which contains the medicine for every illness;
Rejoice, censer of Christ's fragrance, which has poured fragrance over the fallen humanity.
Rejoice, thou who dost liberate the repenting sinner from the ties of sin;
Rejoice, thou who dost abolish the imprisonment of those who strive for purity.
Rejoice, nourishment of virgins and quiet joy of mothers;
Rejoice, Defender of widows and generous care of orphans.
Rejoice, Grace-giving Unconsumed burning Bush, who guards us against fire.

Kontakion 8

It is amazing for us to see how thine icon, Lady, being painted on wood and according to its nature being liable to fire, shows supernatural power and by its presence tames the power of the flames. Realizing God's strength and the power of thy prayers, we all honour the God Creator of All Who extolled thee and granted us, for our joy and comfort thy miracle working image, and Who saves us by this image from fire, so that we may always praise Him gratefully singing: "Alleluia."

Ikos 8

The whole of the Christian world celebrates thy name, most blessed Mary Theotokos, and it is a delight and comfort for every believer to look upon the image of thy countenance, through which thou dost often manifest many glorious miracles. Therefore we, humbly looking at thy holy icon, honour it solemnly and kiss it lovingly, hoping for thy never failing help and protection from it, most of all in times of weakness, when, because of our sins, fire threatens us and, saved by thee from the perishing flames, we cry to thee gratefully:
Rejoice, thou who art the temple of God the Word not made by hand, who excels the Cherubim and who is higher than the Seraphim in holiness and purity;
Rejoice, light raiment of the Sun of Truth, by which the Heavenly Son came to us, who are darkened by sin, to elevate us and take us with Him to Heaven.
Rejoice, thou who hast opened the doors of paradise for the fallen humanity by the holy Nativity;
Rejoice, thou who hast made Heaven and earth sing in choir an unceasing song of praise to thee and to the One born from thee.
Rejoice, Divine source that secreted the water of life that makes those who drink it immortal;
Rejoice, blessed vine that brought forth the Grapes of salvation, which produce the wine of immortality for man.
Rejoice, Grace-giving Unconsumed burning Bush, who guards us against fire.

Kontakion 9

Thy glory, most blessed and celebrated Mother of our God, is above all praise: even the angelic choirs cannot sing a hymn of praise worthy of thee let alone us, made of earth and ashes; but being defeated by our love for thee, we dare to sing to thee, within our powers, a song of praise and gratitude for thy innumerable favours to humankind which thou dost love and for which thou dost care unceasingly, prompting each generation of the faithful to call to Christ the Saviour, born from thee: "Alleluia."

Ikos 9

The eloquent orators are exhausted by their attempts to comprehend the great mystery of thy eternal virginity, which the Lord has concealed from the wisest of this age, but has revealed through their faith to the humble and reverent, who are devoid of inquisitiveness and who confess thee without doubt, in an orthodox way as Virgin before, during and after the Nativity. Thus accept also from us, o Mother and Virgin, our heartfelt confession and strengthen us to follow thine example of chastity and purity of the heart that we may sing to please thee:
Rejoice, snow-white lily of virginity and purity, which blossoms eternally on high;
Rejoice, thou who dost invisibly teach virginity and purity to those living on earth.
Rejoice, thou who hast mysteriously combined in thyself maternity and virginity;
Rejoice, thou who hast preserved thyself in holiness and chastity both bodily and spiritually.
Rejoice, thou who art the leader of monks' assemblies in the purity of soul and body;

Rejoice, Grace-giving Unconsumed burning Bush, who guards us against fire.

Kontakion 10

Wanting to save humankind, One of the Trinity has deigned to become incarnate through thee, God's Bride and Lady, thus glorifying human nature by sitting next to the Father on the right side of God's Throne, as His only-begotten Son. He was also thy Son in the flesh and thus He glorified thee with glory which is higher than any other; being shielded by it thou dost not forget the humankind, because of thy mercy, but thou dost pray to the Creator, One of the Trinity for all who sing to Him a song of praise: "Alleluia."

Ikos 10

Thou art an insuperable defence for the choirs of virgins and the assemblies of monks, Theotokos Virgin, for all who resort to thee through diligent prayer and honour thy holy icon with reverence: for to thee alone God gives the grace of being an intercessor for the entire world and of strengthening the faithful in chastity and purity. Therefore those striving for a chaste life protect themselves against the storms of passions by fleeing to thy motherly protecting Veil and find placidity of the soul, calling unto thee in concert:
Rejoice, firm Protector of the pious monks and nuns and warm Intercessor for them before God;
Rejoice, constant Assistant of God's secret servants in the world and their Instructor in their spiritual practices.
Rejoice, Mentor of chastity and abstention for the young;
Rejoice, delight and comfort of reverent elders.
Rejoice, thou who dost shield the Christian dwellings and families by thy good protecting Veil;

Rejoice, thou who dost vouchsafe each generation of the faithful with thy good care.
Rejoice, Grace-giving Unconsumed burning Bush, who guards us against fire.

Kontakion 11

Christ's holy Church sings to thee an incessant laudatory song, all-praised Lady, proclaiming thy favours and miracles that have enriched the whole universe. Verily, who is more prompt than thee in hearing and fulfilling our entreaties; but thou dost even favour and enrich those in need of thy holy help before they ask for it. Do not deprive us humble ones of this help, now that we sing of the glory of thy name and cry to God: "Alleluia."

Ikos 11

Thy bright icon, most pure Mother of God, enlightens our souls, darkened with sins, by the light of Divine miracles, through which we comprehend the power of God's omnipotence and thine immeasurable mercy, which always is ready to assist us in repentance and conversion from evil deeds to the path of salvation. We beseech thee, all-good Lady, do not let us stray in the maze of sins and passions, but lead us to the quiet refuge of a pious and God pleasing life, that we may offer up to thee our songs of praise:
Rejoice, for demons fear and tremble because of thy holy name;
Rejoice, thou who dost not allow them to possess us by the violence of this mortal body.
Rejoice, for thy glorious icon drives away all devilish powers;

Rejoice, thou who dost strengthen those striving for piety in their battles against the enemies of the salvation of humankind.
Rejoice, thou who dost help those who love and believe thee in the hour of death.
Rejoice, Grace-giving Unconsumed burning Bush, who guards us against fire.

Kontakion 12

We confess that thy holy icon has received God's grace, o blessed Virgin, and we joyfully celebrate the feast of its appearance as the image of the Unconsumed burning Bush. And thine icon confirms it by the miracles it performs, preserving and guarding our dwellings against the flames of fire. Thus having thine icon as a shield and visor, we gratify thee, our mighty Assistant, with songs of praise and we cry to our Saviour Who was born from thee: "Alleluia."

Ikos 12

We sing to thee, Theotokos, our only hope, we tell of thy favours and do not conceal thy miracles, we glorify thine immeasurable goodness to Christians, we bless thy holy name, which is truly like a myrrh for those who love thee, filling the pious souls with spiritual fragrance. Fill with fragrance also us, fouled by spiritual passions, Lady, and vouchsafe us to call to thee with a clean heart and an undefiled mouth:
Rejoice, thou who dost secrete a sweet and soul-saving myrrh, with which God-loving hearts are anointed.
Rejoice thou who dost heal the diseases of body and soul when one just touches thy holy icon.
Rejoice, good Leader, who dost set repenting sinners on the path of a God pleasing life and of salvation;

Rejoice, thou who dost raise Christ's zealots to the gates of the Kingdom of Heaven by the ladder of virtues.
Rejoice, thou who dost crown the humble and patient sufferers with Grace-giving comfort;
Rejoice, thou who dost delight the exiled and those falsely accused by giving them the anticipation of the bliss of paradise.
Rejoice, Grace-giving Unconsumed burning Bush, who guards us against fire.

Kontakion 13

O, all-praised Mother, who gave birth to the most Holy Word and who is called by us, unworthy ones, the "Unconsumed burning Bush": hear our entreaties and songs, which are offered diligently before thy holy icon, and deliver us, by thy warm prayer to the Lord, from the temporary and the eternal fire for we honour thy name and glorify thy miracles, and we cry to thy Son and our God: "Alleluia."
(This Kontakion is read three times, then Ikos 1 and Kontakion 1 should be read.)

Acathistos Hymn

Prayers to the most holy Theotokos before her icon "The Unconsumed burning Bush"

First Prayer

Queen of Heaven, our Lady, Queen of the Universe, most holy Theotokos, undefiled, beyond temptation, imperishable, most pure and always Virgin, Mary, God's Bride, Mother of the Creator of all that is created, the Lord of Glory and the Master of all and everything! Through thee the King of kings and the Lord of lords came to us and appeared on earth. Thou art a personified Divine mercy. Being the Mother of Light and Life, Whom thou once hast born in thy womb and in thy arms thou hast carried Him as the Infant –Pre-eternal Word, thou dost always have Him with thee. Therefore after God thou art our first insuperable defence and intercession and we resort to thee: be merciful and good, all-praised Theotokos, in our fierce bitterness and heal the illnesses of our soul and our body; deliver us from all enemies and villains, deliver us from hunger, exhaustion, curse, from flood and poisonous air, and from a sudden death; and like the three young men in the fiery furnace of Babylon, preserve and protect us, that as in ancient times it was with God's people, all good will come to us, who venerate thee; let our enemies and all those who hate us be put to shame and disgraced, and make them all understand that the Lord is with thee, and through thee God is with us. Shield us in the day by the canopy of thy Grace and in the dark of the night enlighten us by the light from above, giving to all what is useful for them: transform our bitterness into joy and wipe off the tears of thy servants, who have sinned and are now in affliction, fulfil their petitions for what is good, for thou canst fulfil everything thou dost wish, Mother of the Word and of Life. The Father crowned thee as His Daughter, The Son – as Mother Virgin, the Holy Spirit – as

Bride, so that thou dost reign as the Queen, standing on the right side of the Holy Trinity and favour us according to thy will, now and forever and in the ages of ages. Amen

Second Prayer

O most holy and blessed Mother of our sweetest Lord Jesus Christ! We prostrate ourselves and honour thee before thy holy and glorious icon, through which thou dost work amazing and renowned miracles; save our dwellings from fire and lightning, heal the sick and fulfil in a good way our good petitions. We humbly plead with thee, omnipotent Defender of the Christians, vouchsafe us, who are powerless and sinful, with thy Motherly sympathy and care. Save and preserve, Lady, under the veil of thy mercy this dwelling, our Orthodox land (our country) and all of us who kneel before thee with love and faith and with tears ask for thine intercession. O most merciful Lady, take pity on us, seized by many sins and therefore not daring to plead with Christ God for forgiveness, but asking thee, His Mother in the flesh, to be our intercessor. Hold out, o all-good One, thy God-receiving hands, and appeal to His Goodness, asking forgiveness for our transgressions, a pious and peaceful life, a good Christian death and a good defence at His formidable Judgement. And in the time of God's wrath, when our dwellings will be aflame with fire or we will fear lightning and thunder striking us, show us thy gracious protection and invincible help: that saved by thy all-powerful prayers to God we will escape *here* God's temporary punishment and will inherit *there* the eternal bliss of paradise and will sing together with all the saints the most Glorious and Magnificent Name of the worshipped Trinity: the Father, the Son and the Holy Spirit, and thy great mercy to us, in the ages of ages. Amen

Acathistos Hymn

Third Prayer

O most Holy Virgin, the Mother of the Supreme God, the Protectress of all who resort to you. Look from thy holy height onto me the sinner, who prostrates himself before your wonderworking countenance. Hear my humble prayer and bring it to thy beloved Son, our Lord Jesus Christ. Move Him by entreaties so that He would illuminate my gloomy soul by the light of His Divine grace, would free me from any indigence, grief and illness. Let Him grant me with a quiet and peaceful life and both bodily and soul health; let Him quieten my heart full of passions and heal its wounds; let Him teach me to do the good deeds and purify my mind from idle thoughts; let Him teach me to follow His commandments and let Him save me from the eternal torture and may He not close for me the doors of His heavenly Kingdom.

O most holy Mother of God, thou art "the joy of all who sorrow", hear me who is also grieving; thou who art called "the reliever of the sorrow", relieve also my sorrow. Thou art the "The unconsumed burning Bush", protect the world and all of us against the harmful, fiery arrows of the fiend. Thou art the "calling to the account of the fallen ones", do not let me perish in the abyss of my sins. Thou art, after God, my first hope and trust! Be my protector in this transitional life and in eternity and my Intercessor before thy beloved Son and our Lord Jesus Christ. Teach me to serve Him with faith and love and to honour thee piously, the Most holy Mother of God, Mary, full of Grace. I entrust myself to thy holy prayers for the rest of my days. Amen

Fourth Prayer

O most holy Virgin and Mother of God, Queen of Heaven and earth! Hear the sorrowful sigh of our soul; look after us, who faithfully and lovingly honour thy most pure image, from thy holy height. For drowning in our sins and seized by sorrows, gazing at thy image, as if thou really art with us, we offer thee our humble petitions. We have neither another helper, nor intercessor, but thee, the Mother of all the sorrowful and heavy laden. Help us, feeble ones, relieve our grief, and set us, who have strayed, on the right path. Heal and save the hopeless, favour us to spend the rest of our days in peace and stillness, give us a Christian death and be our merciful Defender at the Last Judgement of thy Son, that we may always sing, venerate and glorify thee, as the good Protector of the Christians and all God's servants. O Mother of God, the Unconsumed burning Bush, protect me against the attacks of my fellow men, against the persecution by tyrants, against the eternal fire, against a shameful death, against the eternal torment and shield me by thy heavenly raiment. Amen

Troparion, tone 4

Thou Christ God, Who let Moses see in an unconsumed burning bush Thy most pure Mother, who has received the fire of God in her womb and was unconsumed and who remained virgin after giving birth, we ask Thee: deliver us by her prayers from the fire of passions and spare Thy city from being consumed by fire, for Thou art merciful.

Acathistos Hymn in Honour of the Icon of the Theotokos "The Joy of All Who sorrow"
Celebrated on the 24th October / 6th November

Kontakion 1

To thee, the Victorious Leader, we thy servants, being delivered from wicked people, offer thee Theotokos, our song of gratitude. While thou, having an invincible power, dost shield us in all sorrows and afflictions by thy protecting veil and thy defence and keep us unharmed that we may joyfully call to thee: Rejoice, Grace-giving Virgin who gives joy to all that sorrow.

Ikos 1

The Angel-herald descended from Heaven to thee, pure Virgin, to announce the unspeakable Glad Tidings: that thou would contain in thy womb the One, who is larger than the Heavens. Therefore, amazed at this great mystery, we cry out in praise:
Rejoice, thou who hast received from the angel the Glad Tidings for the entire world;
Rejoice, thou who dost contain in thy womb the One, Whom none and nothing can contain.
Rejoice, thou who hast given birth to the Creator and God of all;
Rejoice, thou who hast been vouchsafed to be His mother;
Rejoice, fulfilment of the Archangel's words;
Rejoice, thou who hast abolished our curse.
Rejoice, thou who hast brought Adam back into paradise;
Rejoice, thou who hast delivered Eve from eternal crying.
Rejoice, liberation from the bonds of hell;
Rejoice, elimination of all delusions.
Rejoice, Grace-giving Virgin who gives joy to all that sorrow.

Kontakion 2

The Lord God having seen the beauty of thy soul, Immaculate Virgin, has chosen thee as the mother of His pre-eternal Son, and thus granted to us, His faithful, a defender for the offended, comfort for the sorrowful, joy for the grieving. Accept, Lady Theotokos, our entreaty for we call on thy name and cry to thy Son and our God: "Alleluia."

Ikos 2

Our mind fails to honour thee properly, who art higher than the Seraphim and more glorious than the Cherubim through the mystery of the Nativity of thy Son and God. It was Him Who conceived the wish to glorify thee and He taught us, who are born on earth, to resort to thy intercession, and with an affectionate heart we cry to thee always:
Rejoice, thou who hast received in thy womb God the Giver of Life to all;
Rejoice, thou who by the Nativity of thy Son hast united God and man.
Rejoice, renewal of the Christian kind;
Rejoice, thou who art our deliverance from perishing.
Rejoice, thou who hast given birth to the One Who is adorned with virtues more than any one;
Rejoice, thou who hast assured us of His favours;
Rejoice, thou who dost shine brighter than the sun;
Rejoice, Mother above all mothers and the most holy one.
Rejoice, thou who dost hear the entreaties of the faithful;
Rejoice, thou who dost provide the poor with never failing bounty.
Rejoice, thou who dost relieve from diseases of the soul and the body;
Rejoice, thou who dost fill our souls with joy.

Rejoice, Grace-giving Virgin who gives joy to all that sorrow.

Kontakion 3

Thou canst ask anything from thy Son and our God for His ear is favourably disposed towards thy entreaties. Thou, Lady, art the Mother of God Who has risen from the dead and ascended to heaven and Who vouchsafed us on earth, to sing about thee to God: "Alleluia."

Ikos 3

Thou art, Lady Theotokos, a faithful Intercessor for our salvation. Thou alone art endowed by thy Son and our God with the Grace-giving gift: to pour out thy favours and to save and defend us in all our sorrows, misfortunes and afflictions. Therefore we cry to thee gratefully:
Rejoice, thou who art the Queen of queens and the merciful Mother of mothers;
Rejoice, most reliable Defender of our kind.
Rejoice, thou who dost stand before the throne of the King of all and God;
Rejoice, thou who dost pray to Him for us.
Rejoice, thou who dost hold out thy hands towards thy Son and our God;
Rejoice, thou who dost offer up to Him our prayers.
Rejoice, thou who dost protect those who faithfully resort to thee in all circumstances;
Rejoice, thou who dost inspire in our souls humility and meekness.
Rejoice, thou who dost turn God's wrath into favour;
Rejoice, thou who dost turn our sorrows into joy.
Rejoice, our deliverance from afflictions and misfortunes;
Rejoice, thou who dost promptly heal the sick.

Rejoice, Grace-giving Virgin who gives joy to all that sorrow.

Kontakion 4

The storm of many sorrows, misfortunes and afflictions comes upon us, and we, being feeble, are not able to endure them because of our sins, and we do not have another healer, but thee, o Immaculate Theotokos! Nothing is impossible for thee and if thou dost wish thou canst deliver us from afflictions and save us, who resort to thee faithfully and affectionately, and pray to thee and cry in tears to God: "Alleluia."

Ikos 4

The Lord hears thy motherly prayer for us, and He accepts it and fulfils all thy requests. While we, having seen the inexhaustible precipice of thy merciful healing of souls and bodies, dare to sing to thee:
Rejoice, thou who art the medicine against our passions, by which we are healed;
Rejoice, thou who art the hope for the eternal good, by which we strengthen ourselves.
Rejoice, thou whose prayer gives us life and nourishment;
Rejoice, thou whose favours delight us more than the honeycomb.
Rejoice, golden censer of the Divine Coal;
Rejoice, thou who dost preserve the spiritual fragrance in our souls.
Rejoice, thou who dost subside the waves of sin;
Rejoice, thou who dost illuminate our souls to seek salvation.
Rejoice, thou who dost teach wisdom to the unwise;
Rejoice, thou who dost strengthen the infants.
Rejoice, thou who dost set back on the right path those who were led astray;

Rejoice, thou who by thy prayer dost amend all those deprived of God's mercy.
Rejoice, Grace-giving Virgin who gives joy to all that sorrow.

Kontakion 5

A Divine star has revealed the Lord God to us: thou, whom He has chosen as His Mother and who hears the entreaties of all on earth. Every choir in heaven and on earth gratifies thee, Immaculate Mother of Christ our God, therefore, we, the sinners, knowing thee as a prompt Defender against all evil attacks, sorrows and illnesses, cry to God gratefully for these gifts: "Alleluia."

Ikos 5

Seeing the multitude of thy miracles, how thou dost heal the sick, drive out demons from the possessed and protect us all against offences, we cry to thee:
Rejoice, star that adorns the heavens better than the sun;
Rejoice, thou who dost comfort our souls by obtaining from God forgiveness for our sins.
Rejoice, thou who dost bring to God the prayers of those who pray to thee;
Rejoice, thou who dost fulfil the requests brought to thee.
Rejoice, joy of those in sorrow;
Rejoice, only refuge for the sad.
Rejoice, prompt defender in misfortunes and sorrows;
Rejoice, healing from all diseases.
Rejoice, warding off of unexpected disasters;
Rejoice, deliverance from slander.
Rejoice, for we all are being delivered from the eternal torment;

Rejoice, thou who dost admonish us for the salvation of our souls.
Rejoice, Grace-giving Virgin who gives joy to all that sorrow.

Kontakion 6

After the church in thy holy name, Mother of God, had been erected, and the Evangelist Luke brought thee the portrait he had painted of thy most pure countenance, the preachers of the universe, the God-bearing Apostles invited thee there for the ceremony of consecration. But thou spake to them: go in peace and I will be there with you. Having entered the church the Apostles found on the wall the image of thy countenance, not made by human hands: being amazed at such a miracle, falling on our knees, we call to God: "Alleluia."

Ikos 6

God's grace shines before us: the image of thy most pure countenance not made by hands, Lady Virgin Theotokos. For thou thyself, looking at thy first painted icon, said: "My Grace and my strength be with this icon forever" and thy words came true because of thy power. Therefore we cry to thee the following laudatory song:
Rejoice, thou who art an inexhaustible sea of God's grace;
Rejoice, thou who art the immeasurable depth of His mercy.
Rejoice, thou who dost hold sway over the entire world;
Rejoice, defender of the Christian kind.
Rejoice, invincible defence of the Church;
Rejoice, thou who art praised by the pious clerics.
Rejoice, candle that illuminated us with the light of dawn;
Rejoice, thou who dost instruct us to follow the path of salvation.
Rejoice, hope of the hopeless;

Rejoice, thou who dost call to account the fallen ones.
Rejoice, prompt deliverance from afflictions;
Rejoice, joyful comfort of the sorrowful.
Rejoice, Grace-giving Virgin who gives joy to all that sorrow.

Kontakion 7

Thou dost save and guard against evil attacks those who with faith visit thy holy temple and look with joy in their hearts on thy miracle working and holy icon, where thy mercy towards those asking for help is portrayed. Therefore, we also call to thee affectionately: O most blessed Lady! Give us, who grieve in our afflictions, joy; heal the diseased that we may diligently cry to the God of all about thee: "Alleluia."

Ikos 7

Thou hast shown the manciple Theophilos the path of repentance and how to return to God the Creator of all, after he had turned away from Him and from thee, but then he repented and prayed in thy temple before thine icon, for thou art the Defender of the Christian kind. And thou, Virgin, hast accepted his repentance and fulfilled his petitions. Accept, Lady, also our entreaty and do not neglect us, who sing to thee:
Rejoice, thou who dost fulfil our petitions;
Rejoice, thou who dost delight us when we suffer in soul and body.
Rejoice, thou who dost give food to the hungry;
Rejoice, inexhaustible drink for the thirsty.
Rejoice, for through thee the deaf become able to hear;
Rejoice, for through thee the blind become able to see.
Rejoice, clothes of all the naked and indigent;
Rejoice, strengthening of all the exhausted.

Rejoice, thou who dost guard us against disasters and illnesses;
Rejoice, thou who dost give hope to the desperate.
Rejoice, Grace-giving Virgin who gives joy to all that sorrow.

Kontakion 8

The appearance of thy miracle working icon, most pure Mother of God, is most amazing for us, for it was carried in the air by God's Grace. What could possibly make thee manifest thyself in such a wondrous way, except thy motherly care for us? Therefore we pray to thee: visit us, who are sinful, who suffer in our afflictions, sorrows and illnesses that we dare to sing to God the angels' hymn: "Alleluia."

Ikos 8

Truly all people have praised the miracles of thy holy icon, for the multitude of the faithful from all countries and cities resort to it, bringing their prayers, and in return being healed of their diseases: thou art the joy of all that sorrow. Therefore, honouring the day of the appearance of thy holy icon, we dare to cry to thee a song of praise:
Rejoice, Keeper of the Christian kind;
Rejoice, our faithful Protector.
Rejoice, thou who dost hear our prayers;
Rejoice, thou who dost shield us by thy protecting veil.
Rejoice, thou who dost feed us in our hunger;
Rejoice, thou who dost deliver us from flood and sinking.
Rejoice, thou who dost guard us against terror and earthquake;
Rejoice, thou who dost provide us with everything we need.
Rejoice, our help in afflictions and disasters;
Rejoice, joyful consolation in our sorrows.

Rejoice, thou who dost gladden the grieving who pray to thee;
Rejoice, thou who dost comfort our souls with the delight of the Kingdom of Heaven.
Rejoice, Grace-giving Virgin who gives joy to all that sorrow.

Kontakion 9

All the angels fly together to the Throne of the King on High, and standing in fear, listen to thy prayer for us, sinners, to Thy Son and our God, for He fulfils all thy petitions. Therefore we pray to thee, o Mother of God, who has the gift to ward off diseases and deliver from sorrows and afflictions: inspire us to sing always about thee to God: "Alleluia."

Kontakion 10

Wishing to save the entire world, the Lord has promised eternal life to us all; but we, being sinful, have a darkened mind and do not observe His commandments, for which we deserve His formidable Judgement and punishment; no one will be able to help us, but thee, the Mother of God on High. Prostrating ourselves before thee, we pray: accept, Lady, our entreaties and dispose thy Son and our God favourably that He may deliver us from the eternal torments, from any temporary malicious and fierce attack of our visible and invisible enemies and from all the sorrows which hamper us, singing about thee to the God of all: "Alleluia."

Ikos 9

Eloquent orators do not know how worthily to praise thy greatness, all-blessed Theotokos, as thou dost guard the entire world against all slander and evil attacks: therefore, in our innocence we dare cry lovingly to thee:
Rejoice, thou who art a powerful help in battles;
Rejoice, thou who dost strengthen the Christian host.

Rejoice, thou who dost protect the world by silence;
Rejoice, thou who dost strengthen the helpless.
Rejoice, thou who dost relieve all sorrow;
Rejoice, thou who dost heal the sick.
Rejoice, thou who dost destroy the nets of the cunning ones;
Rejoice, thou who dost guard us against evil people.
Rejoice, thou who dost deliver us from afflictions and misfortunes;
Rejoice, thou who dost instruct our souls on how to find salvation.
Rejoice, Grace-giving Virgin who gives joy to all that sorrow.

Kontakion 10

Wishing to save the entire world, the Lord has promised eternal life to us all; but we, being sinful, have a darkened mind and do not observe His commandments, for which we deserve His formidable Judgement and punishment; no one will be able to help us, but thee, the Mother of God on High. Prostrating ourselves before thee, we pray: accept, Lady, our entreaties and dispose thy Son and our God favourably that He may deliver us from the eternal torments, from any temporary malicious and fierce attack of our visible and invisible enemies and from all the sorrows which hamper us, singing about thee to the God of all: "Alleluia."

Ikos 10

Thou art an invincible defender and protector of the faithful, most merciful Intercessor: protect, shield and keep us: thy motherly prayers are a great help to us, who are lost and powerless. Thou canst obtain by asking anything from thy Son and our God; therefore we cry to thee:
Rejoice, the only merciful Mother;

Rejoice, intercessor for our salvation.
Rejoice, for through thee joy is given to the world;
Rejoice, thou who dost pour in our souls the heavenly delight.
Rejoice, for thou dost expose any lie, hidden in cunning words;
Rejoice, thou who dost ruin the councils of evil.
Rejoice, thou who dost guard against the visible and invisible enemies;
Rejoice, trustworthy rescue of those drowning.
Rejoice, thou who dost help in all sorrows and needs;
Rejoice, thou who dost visit the sick.
Rejoice, Grace-giving Virgin who gives joy to all that sorrow.

Kontakion 11

We, thy servants, bring our song and our grateful prayers to thee, Theotokos: thou art the protector of the human kind. Take care of us, the helpless, and by thy prayer to God subdue His anger which falls upon us and obtain from Him our deliverance from all fierce sorrow and illness, that we also may cry to Him, our God: "Alleluia."

Ikos 11

The candle which was kindled by the burning coal of God's Grace, has appeared to illuminate and to save our souls. Therefore we, lovingly honouring the day of thy celebration and praising thy miracles, dare to cry to thee:
Rejoice, strength of orthodox kings;
Rejoice, giver of the victory in battles.
Rejoice, conqueror of all enemies;
Rejoice, thou who dost guard us from internecine strife.
Rejoice, glory of the orthodox;
Rejoice, chastity of those preserving their virginity.

Rejoice, shield by which we defend ourselves against our enemies;
Rejoice, thou who dost deliver us promptly from afflictions and sorrows.
Rejoice, quiet refuge of those seized by passions;
Rejoice, prompt and miraculous healing of the sick.
Rejoice, our invincible defence;
Rejoice, our hope and protection on the Day of Judgement.
Rejoice, Grace-giving Virgin who gives joy to all that sorrow.

Kontakion 12

By the Grace given to thee by the Supreme God, thou hast given thine icon as a refuge for the faithful; therefore we honour thee alone, our Lady Theotokos and always Virgin, our prompt and trustworthy intercessor in afflictions, sorrows and diseases and in great joy we sing about thee to God: "Alleluia."

Ikos 12

Firmly establish the minds of those that hymn thee, Immaculate Virgin, the strong defender of the entire world; help us by thy prayers for afflictions come upon us, our sorrows multiply and our enemies take up arms against us. Conquer our enemies, let all who do evil to us be disgraced. Therefore we diligently call to thee, crying:
Rejoice, Mother chosen from all generations once and for all;
Rejoice, thou who dost shield all men with thy protecting veil.
Rejoice, thou who dost shed a mother's tears for us;
Rejoice, thou who dost wash away our sins.
Rejoice, thou who dost clothe our souls with the raiment of immortality;
Rejoice, thou who art our helper in every need.

Rejoice, thou who dost heal the distress of soul and body;
Rejoice, thou who dost give us the bread of life when we hunger.
Rejoice, for we enjoy thy favours;
Rejoice, thou who dost make us better.
Rejoice, thou who dost teach us repentance;
Rejoice, thou who dost help sinners on the terrible Day of Judgement.
Rejoice, Grace-giving Virgin who gives joy to all that sorrow.

Kontakion 13

O all-praised Mother, who gave birth to Christ, our God, hear the lamentation of thy grieving servants! We fasten our gaze on thee, we hold out our hands to thee and we call to thee from the depth of our souls: accept this small entreaty from us, blessed Lady, Queen, and be merciful to us: deliver us from afflictions, sorrows and misfortunes; heal our ailments, destroy the slander about us and do not let us perish from hunger, earthquake, flood and sudden death, for we cry tearfully to God: "Alleluia."
(This Kontakion is read three times, and then Ikos 1 and Kontakion 1 should be read.)

The prayers to the most holy Theotokos before her icon "The Joy of All Who sorrow"

First prayer

O most holy Theotokos, higher than the Cherubim and more glorious than the Seraphim, who gave birth to Christ, our God, great amazement of angels, fulfilment of the prophecy, Maid chosen by God, joy of all that sorrow, defender of the offended, who nourishes those who hunger, refuge of those seized by passions, visitor of the sick, protecting veil and defence of the powerless, protector of the orphans, haven for those sailing, companion of the travellers, rest for those who labour, clothes for the naked, inexhaustible richness of the poor, quiet gladness of the mothers, strength of the infants, unfailing help of the helpless, true protector of the Christians. O most merciful Virgin, Lady Theotokos! To thee alone has been given the gift of Grace from the Most High to defend and to save us in all afflictions. O all-praised Mother, Virgin Theotokos! Hear the entreaties of thy servants who stand before thy miracle working icon; and looking at it, we see thee as if thou art alive, Theotokos, and prostrate ourselves before thee with our souls full of faith and love and boldly cry to thee with the words of the psalm: "Hearken, O daughter, and consider, and incline thine ear" (Ps. 45:10); hear our entreaty, for thou hast heard the entreaties of the faithful in their afflictions; all plead with thee in their sorrows, for thou art strong, asking help, deliverance and defence. And thou, being the joy of all that sorrow, fulfil the petitions of the sorrowful and delight their souls with joy. O merciful and most merciful Lady, Queen Theotokos. Thou canst obtain by thy entreaties anything at all from thy Son, Christ, our God: do not withdraw thy protection from us, o Immaculate Virgin, deliver us from our sorrows and afflictions, from our visible and invisible enemies and the wicked men who slander us; do not let hunger, earthquake, flood, fire and sword come upon us; be our persistent assistant and plead with thy Son and our God that He would count us as those standing at His right hand on the fearful Judgement Day, because of thy intercession. To Him we give glory and worship, together with His Father without begin and the Holy Spirit, now and always and unto the ages of ages. Amen

Second Prayer

O most holy Virgin, Mother of Christ our God, Queen of Heaven and earth, hear the painful sighs of our souls, take care of us from thy holy height, for we faithfully and lovingly honour thy most chaste image. Being burdened by our sins and seized by sorrows, gazing at thy image we bring to thee our humble entreaties, for we do not have any other help, intercession and consolation but thee, o Mother of all the grieving and heavy laden, help us, who are powerless, relieve our sorrow, set us who stray on the right path, heal our ill hearts and save us, who are hopeless. Grant us to accomplish the rest of our life in peace and repentance, give us a Christian death and be our merciful intercessor at the Last Judgement of Thy Son, that we may always hymn, honour and glorify thee as a good defender of the Christian kind, together with all God's servants. Amen.

* * *

The History of the Icons

1. "She who mollifies the wicked hearts"

The icon of the Mother of God "She who mollifies the wicked hearts" is also called "Simeon's Prophecy". As the evangelist Luke narrates, the righteous elder Simeon was told by the Holy Spirit that he wouldn't die until he had seen the Messiah. And when after forty days, Josef and Mary brought the Infant Jesus to the Temple of Jerusalem, Simeon, inspired by the Holy Spirit, also went there. He took the Infant in his arms and said the famous words, which are known as the prayer of Saint Simeon-The God-receiver and are said at the end of Vespers: "Lord, now lettest thou thy servant depart in peace, according to thy word" (Luke 2:29).

Then he blessed Josef and the most pure Mother of the Saviour and he prophesied to her: "Behold, this child is set for the fall and rising again of many in Israel; and for a sign which shall be spoken against; Yea, a sword shall pierce through thy own soul also, that the thoughts of many hearts may be revealed" (Luke 2:34-35).

As Christ's hands and body were pierced by the nails and the spear, so the soul of His mother will be pierced by the sword of sadness and pain of the heart when she will watch the suffering of her Son: and then the hidden thoughts of the people, who must make the choice: are they with Christ or against Him, will be revealed.

This exegesis of Simeon's prophecy has become the subject of several "symbolical" icons of the Theotokos. All who have been praying to them have felt that when the heart becomes mollified it becomes easier to bear the suffering of soul and body. And when they pray before these icons for their enemies, then the feeling of hostility becomes less strong and gives way to mercy; the internecine enmity subsides.

This icon probably comes from South-West Russia; however this is not confirmed by history.
Usually in this icon the Theotokos is painted with the swords that pierce her heart: three swords on the left and three on the right side and one sword from below. The number "seven" symbolises in the Holy Script fullness, completeness: thus it symbolises in this particular case the fullness of the Theotokos' grief during her earthly life.

The feast of this icon takes place during the Week of all Saints (the first Sunday after Pentecost).

2. "The Increase of Intelligence"

On the 15th / 28th August the feast in honour of the icon of Mother of God "The Increase of Intelligence" is celebrated.

According to tradition this icon was painted in the 17th century by an icon painter who suffered from amnesia and attacks of insanity. He had a vision of the Mother of God, who commanded him to paint her icon in the way we see it now, and the icon painter was healed.

The prototype of this icon is the statue of the Mother of God in the Italian city Loreto. This connection was discovered by the Russian palaeographer A. A. Titov at the beginning of the 20th century.

The Mother of God and Christ are depicted in this icon as enveloped together by the phelonios, the ritual outer garment of the Orthodox priest.
They are wearing royal crowns. Christ holds in His left hand the orb. In the upper part of the icon the arch is depicted which symbolises the gate and at the bottom of the icon the houses which symbolise the Kingdom of Heaven. Above the Mother of God, three seraphim soar and there is one cherub at her feet.

The following inscription can often be found at the bottom of the icon:
"The image of the Most Holy Theotokos to judge the living and the dead: it guards against murderers, pernicious winds, shivers, fits, attacks by poisonous creatures, enemies, midges and mosquitoes.

3. "The Protective Veil of the Most Holy Theotokos"

"The Protective Veil of the Most Holy Theotokos" is mainly celebrated in Russian Orthodoxy and is considered to be one of the Great Feasts. It is celebrated on 1st / 14th October.

The feast came into being in honour of the appearance of the Most Holy Theotokos in the church of the Blachernae in Constantinople in 910.

In the days of the emperor Leo the Wise and patriarch Macarios, a joint army of the Russian dukes under the guidance of duke Oleg the Prophet was approaching Constantinople.
On Sunday, October 1st the church of the Blachernae was full of believers who were attending the all-night vigil. They prayed after the service to the Mother of God, pleading her to defend them against the attackers. Blessed Andrew, the theologian and the fool in Christ, of Slavonic origin, who was also present there together with his disciple Epiphanios, the future Patriarch of Constantinople, suddenly had a marvellous vision of the Mother of God.

Illuminated by the unearthly, uncreated light she walked in the air from the west doors of the church, accompanied by a throng of prophets, apostles, angels, who were glorifying the most Pure One, towards the altar. Next to her two saints were walking: John the Baptist and John the Theologian. She

entered the altar, kneeled there and prayed for all the Christians.
"Do you see, brother, the Queen and the Lady of all, who prays for us?" Andrew the fool in Christ asked his disciple. "I see, holy father, and I tremble," Epiphanios replied.

Then they both saw the Theotokos take off her veil, which shone like lightning, and spread it above the praying people. And the veil became so huge that it covered the entire Christian world. "Do you see, brother?" "Yes I do, father".
And suddenly the Russians retreated, after Oleg the Prophet had nailed his shield to the gates of Constantinople. It happened a century before Russia accepted Christianity.

This event, which meant the defeat of the Russians, is now celebrated by the Russian Orthodox Church as the feast of the protection by the Mother of God of all Orthodox Christians. This feast was established in 1160 by the Russian Prince Andrew the God-lover who also built the first church in the name of the Protective Veil of the Mother of God on the river Nerl.

4. "Hodigitria"

Hodigitria (She who shows the Way) – is one of the most widely spread types of the images of the Theotokos with the

Infant Jesus, painted according to Church lore, by the Evangelist Luke.

The Infant Jesus sits on the Theotokos' lap: with His right hand he blesses, and in His left hand he holds a manuscript, or more seldom a book, which corresponds to the iconographic type of Christ Pantocrator (The Ruler of all). As a rule, the Theotokos is represented in a half-length portrait; however there are also shortened portraits, to the shoulders (the Mother of God of Kazan) and full-length portraits.

In this icon Jesus is the centre of the composition looking at the spectators, and the Theotokos stresses it as she points at Jesus with her right hand.
From the dogmatic point of view the meaning of this image is the coming into the world of the "heavenly king and judge" and the worshipping of the royal child. On the contrary, the type of icon of the Theotokos which is called "Eleusa" (Tenderness or Showing mercy) expresses mainly the limitless love of the Theotokos for her Divine Son.

According to the church tradition the first Hodigitria (The icon of Blachernae) was painted by the evangelist Luke. About the middle of the fifth century Eudokia, the wife of the Emperor Theodosius, brought this icon to Constantinople and placed it in the church of the Blachernae (according to another source it was placed in the Convent Odigon, which name has contributed to the later name of the icon: Hodigitria). The icon became the most sacred object and the defender of Constantinople. When enemies besieged the city, the icon was brought out to the walls in a solemn procession. Besides such special occasions, every Tuesday the icon was carried in procession through the streets of the entire city.

This type of icon of the Mother of God has become widely known in the entire Christian world, and in Byzantium and Russia in particular.

5. "Unfading Blossom"

On the 3rd /16th April the Russian Church celebrates the feast in honour of the icon of the Mother of God "Unfading Blossom".

In this icon the Mother of God holds her Divine Son on her right arm, while in her left hand she holds a white lily. This flower symbolises the virginity and chastity of the Most Pure Theotokos, whom the Holy Church praises: "Thou art the root of virginity and the Unfading Blossom of purity." The first icon of this type was created in the Western school of painting, and it was lost in the course of time.

In Russia this type of icon appeared in the 18th century through pilgrims.
Believers pray before it asking for chastity, purity and righteousness and also, help to find a good spouse.

The Mother of God "Unfading Blossom" helps finding spiritual strength to overcome ordeals, the continuation of life and fulfilment of the Christian duty.

6. "The Unconsumed Burning Bush"

The wonderworking icon of the Mother of God "The unconsumed Burning Bush" is composed on the basis of the principal prophesies of the Old Testament about the incarnation of Christ and reveals several aspects of its worshipping.

The Mother of God and the Infant are in the centre of the icon. In her hands the Mother of God holds a number of symbols from the prophecies: the Mountain from Daniel's prophecy, Jacob's ladder, Ezekiel's Gates and so on. The representations of the Mother of God and the Infant are enclosed in an eight-pointed star, which is formed by two squares, a green and a red one. The green one symbolises the Bush, and the red one symbolises the Divine Fire which burned in it. Around the star, Old Testament scenes are depicted: Moses standing before the Burning Bush, the dream of Jacob, the Gates of Ezekiel and the Tree of Jesse.

Another theme of this icon is that of the Angel serving the Mother of God and the heavenly powers honouring the miraculous birth of God from a Virgin. The angels are painted inside the rays of the eight-pointed star. Amongst them there are archangels and nameless angels, the embodiments of the elements, known from the Commentary on the Old Testament, the Book of Enoch and other apocryphal works.

The icon "Unconsumed burning Bush" is honoured as a mighty defender against fire.
The feast of this icon is celebrated on 4th / 17th September.

7. "The Joy of All Who sorrow"

"The Joy of All Who sorrow" is the first line of one of the of hymns of the Theotokos. The first icon of this name is now known only by the records in the archives and was painted in 1683 by the court painter Ivan Bezmin, who worked in the European style.

This type of Russian icon was inspired by West-European painting: Madonna in Gloria, Misericordia, Immaculate Conception of the Virgin Mary. The Orthodox icons which influenced it were: "The Life-giving Spring, Tenderness and Visiting of Those suffering in afflictions".

Next to the representation of the Theotokos, it includes traditionally the representations of men and women suffering from illnesses, and angels, who accomplish good deeds on behalf of the Theotokos. She is portrayed in full length, surrounded by a mandorla (radiance) with the Infant on her right arm, but mostly without Him. Above her, in the clouds the Lord Sabaoth is represented or the Trinity of the New Testament. The Virgin Mary stands on the crescent (Rev.

12:1) or on the clouds. In her hands she holds a prayer rope, manuscript or bread.
The feast of this icon is celebrated on 24th October / 6th Nomeber

www.ingramcontent.com/pod-product-compliance
Lightning Source LLC
LaVergne TN
LVHW041849070526
838199LV00045BB/1519